Making 'Birth to three matters' work for you

by

Helen M. Rowlands
and staff at Hope Park Community Nursery, Liverpool

A QEd Publication

Published in 2005

© Helen M. Rowlands

ISBN 1 898873 42 9

British Library Cataloguing
A catalogue record for this book is available from the British Library.

Published by QEd Publications, 39 Weeping Cross, Stafford ST17 0DG
Tel: 01785 620364
Website: www.qed.uk.com
Email: orders@qed.uk.com

Cover photographs by Rachel Fletcher (rachelfletcherphotography@yahoo.co.uk)
Printed in the United Kingdom by FOLIUM Group Ltd.

Contents

Introduction

Birth to three matters. A framework to support children in their earliest years (Sure Start, 2003) provides support and guidance for those working with children aged between birth and 36 months. This manual is intended to be used in conjunction with the framework and offers practical hints, tips and sample activities to help give you a real head start. Developed by Helen M. Rowlands, it draws on her experience as a nursery nurse and offers insights into how the framework was put into practice at Hope Park Community Nursery in Liverpool, where she has been nursery manager for more than 18 years.

In this introductory section a number of sample activities have been prepared to help individuals or groups get to grips with using this manual. These exercises will provide valuable training sessions in understanding how the framework really works and how to plan meaningful activities for the children in your care. The exercises have been tried and tested in many nursery settings and we feel confident that because of their very simplicity childcare staff will find them invaluable.

Throughout the section the ☞ symbol has been used to indicate a practical activity. Tick the box on the right when you have completed it to help you keep track of your progress.

Putting the manual into practice

Take some time to look through the manual and you will find that the core principles are the same throughout each section. There are sample activity sheets illustrating ways of applying each individual Component. At the end of each section there are blank activity sheets. In this introductory section you will be shown how to complete your own activity sheets and slot them into your planning. This means that there is no need for you to read slavishly through the entire manual, simply select an age group that you will be working with and focus on applying the framework to a child in that group. Once you are confident that you understand the implications with regards to that one child, transfer the framework to others in the age group. Once you have done this, and identified the differences inherent in the group, you should then look further and apply the same principles to another child from a different age group. Remember to move to the appropriate aged section and you will find that everything slots into place very comfortably.

In order to simplify the use of gender, we have alternated fairly loosely between male and female throughout the manual.

Because it is usual that practitioners work alongside one or two others closely, as well as additional practitioners in neighbouring age groups, I would suggest that introducing this method at a training session with your under threes team will have the most beneficial effect. I have continued in this section with a suggested outline for your workshop, but of course you may choose to follow this in isolation until you feel comfortable enough to continue.

Where to start?

As you are aware, the framework is separated into four age groups:

- Heads Up, Lookers and Communicators (0–8 months)
- Sitters, Standers and Explorers (8–18 months)
- Movers, Shakers and Players (18–24 months)
- Walkers, Talkers and Pretenders (24–36 months)

For explanatory purposes, the second age group, Sitters, Standers and Explorers, is going to be used throughout this section, so you might like to start by copying those pages now.

Each age group is subdivided into four Aspects. These are:

- A Strong Child
- A Skilful Communicator
- A Competent Learner
- A Healthy Child

These Aspects are further subdivided into four Components:

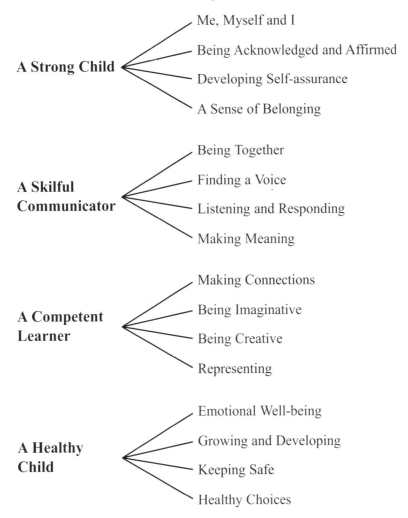

A Strong Child
- Me, Myself and I
- Being Acknowledged and Affirmed
- Developing Self-assurance
- A Sense of Belonging

A Skilful Communicator
- Being Together
- Finding a Voice
- Listening and Responding
- Making Meaning

A Competent Learner
- Making Connections
- Being Imaginative
- Being Creative
- Representing

A Healthy Child
- Emotional Well-being
- Growing and Developing
- Keeping Safe
- Healthy Choices

To ensure that our record-keeping and planning can be as simple as possible, a simple code has been allocated to each of the components throughout the framework. You will find a code list at the end of each section, but of course there is no need for you to memorise them. Simply take out the relevant page as you prepare your planner for easy reference.

	Activity	Tick when completed
☞	In the manual, key areas of each of the Components are listed so take a little while now to familiarise yourself with the pages referring to the Strong Child of the section you have separated. There is no need at this point to go over the Sample Activity pages.	
☞	Once you have done this, photocopy pages 6 and 7.	
☞	Gather together a pencil or crayon in each of four colours – purple, pink, green and blue. Collect a yellow highlighter too. Read 'A day in the life of Tilly Mint' and using your purple crayon *lightly* colour over the parts of Tilly's day that you feel reflect a Strong Child.	

A day in the life of Tilly Mint, aged 14 months

Time	Activity	Achieved
8:00	Tilly arrives at nursery with her mum who passes over the terry towelling nappies. Tilly is happy to see her key worker Sue and waves goodbye to mum easily. Sue helps Tilly build a house with the Mega Blocks.	
8:45	As the babies move through in to their own location, Tilly is holding Sue's hand, but pulling her through, keen to get to her own room. Sue sits Tilly down at the table, encouraging her to choose her own bib and try to put it on herself, offering a helping hand.	
9:00	Sheila brings in toast and jam for the morning snack and before the plates are ready Tilly is holding out her hand saying 'Ta' to Sarah who is nearest to the toast.	
9:30	While other staff tidy away the snack, Sue gets out a guitar that she has brought to nursery and Phil begins to play. Tilly is immediately interested in this and goes over to investigate. Phil shows her how to strum the strings and she is clearly impressed at the sounds she can make. Jeanette gets more musical instruments out and before long most of the group has joined in. Tilly goes from one instrument to another while she tries them out and ends up dancing for herself.	
10:45	After a brief interlude with a different selection of toys it is time for Tilly's group to visit the Sensory Room. She walks down the corridor by herself, leading the way to get there quicker. Phil is by her side but Tilly prefers not to hold her hand and walk under her own steam. In the Sensory Room, Sue selects the projected images of under the sea and Tilly enjoys following the moving images across the floor for more than 10 minutes, but then instantly dismisses them and runs around the room shouting loudly to hear her own voice. She plays independently with different equipment but stops regularly to check that she is still being watched and laughs when she knows that she has somebody's attention.	
11:15	Session over, it is time to walk back to the room for a nappy change and to get ready for lunch. Tilly is not quite so anxious to return and lags behind the group, eventually sitting down on the floor in protest at having to leave. Sue picks her up with a laugh to soften her thunderous expression and Tilly soon softens. Taking her straight into the nappy change Sue can sense that Tilly is getting tired and will need livening up if she is to enjoy dinner and pudding before falling asleep. Sue tickles her tummy and makes her laugh while getting her changed.	
11:30	Today's lunch is shepherd's pie with beetroot, which is brought in on plates to cool down. Again Tilly puts on her own bib and tries to get Phil's attention because she is nearest to the lunch. As soon as she has her plate in front of her, Tilly tucks in using her spoon and her fingers to push it on. When all of her group have their lunch Sue sits with them and asks if anybody would like her help. Asking Tilly directly, Tilly refuses to give Sue her spoon to help so Sue lets her get on with it. Watching her closely she offers more help as Tilly gets frustrated that she can't pick anything else up from the bowl. This time she lets Sue help her finish off her shepherd's pie. As her lunch bowl is collected by Jeanette, Tilly objects as Sue wipes her face and hands with a clean cloth in preparation for pudding which arrives almost instantly. Carrot cake is another of Tilly's favourites and she eats it very quickly.	
12:10	After another wipe of her face and hands, Tilly is ready for her afternoon nap. Despite numerous attempts by Sue and other key staff, Tilly does not like to go to sleep on the floor cushions or in a cot. Instead she prefers to go to sleep in a buggy so Sue makes her comfortable, wheeling her up and down in the darkened room until she has dropped off. After a short while Tilly can be moved to a floor cushion where she will sleep longer than if she had stayed in the buggy. She is moved carefully, covered with her blanket and given her teddy to hug without her even batting an eyelid.	

Time	Activity	Achieved
1:45	Tilly sleeps longer than normal today and wakes in a very good mood. For a little while she is happy playing with the large wooden toys that have been set out but soon spots a group of older children playing outside. Going over to the door she bangs loudly, saying 'Out! Out!' to anybody who will listen.	
2:00	Phil brings in a small pile of coats belonging to the older babies and asks Tilly which is her coat. Tilly immediately identifies her coat and gives it to Phil to put on. As soon as her coat is on she stands impatiently at the door again shouting 'Out!' while she waits for the others in her group to have their coats put on. Door opens and she is raring to go. While outside she plays football, runs up and down the patio a great deal and bangs on the windows of other rooms to attract the attention of other children.	
2:30	Back inside she is ready for something calm so Phil asks her group 'Would you like a story?' Although she is not in Phil's group Tilly simply takes a seat with the group and enjoys *My Jungle* with the other group. Tilly thoroughly enjoys the book, making verbal comment about the pop-up animals and bright pictures. She remains sitting still while the book is read again, joining in slightly more than the first reading. After this Phil encourages the children to sit with their own books and they all sit happily and read the board books that they are given.	
3:00	Time for afternoon snack and Sheila has arrived with cheese and crackers. Without any instruction Tilly goes over to the table but finds no chairs. Instinctively she goes over to the milk kitchen and bangs at Sue, who she can see through the window. Sue gets the message and helps Tilly to put a chair at the table, asking her 'Where shall I put it? Do you want to sit by Andrew?' Tilly indicates where she would like to sit by pointing next to Jack and sits on the chair immediately. She enjoys her snack, needing no help at all, and almost helping Jack to finish off his before he spots her.	
3:30	After snack time there is a selection of coloured pencils and coloured paper laid out on the tables and Duplo on the floor. Tilly selects a handful of pencils and makes her marks on the paper with all of the pencils at the same time. Looking at her picture she is clearly pleased with her result and gathers a handful of pencils in the other hand too, making her marks on the paper with both hands at the same time. She gets fed up very quickly and drops the pencils, watching as some of them roll off the table and onto the floor. She sits playing with the Duplo, building a tower with Sue until her mum and dad arrive at 4:00.	
4:00	Sitting playing happily, for a minute or two Tilly is unaware that her parents have arrived. Sue smiles to them but does not draw Tilly's attention to them so that they can watch her play for a while. As soon as they are spotted any building plans are forgotten and she runs as far away as possible so that Dad has to chase her to put her coat on. This gives Mum a chance to ask Sue about her day, and Sue gives her lots of feedback before they leave for the afternoon.	

What next?

You may find that you have coloured in quite a lot of the text, but don't worry. Because the framework encompasses many of the ordinary but vital parts of a child's development it is natural that there will be some overlap.

Some of these examples might help you to check that you are on the right track:

- At 3:00pm Tilly indicates that she would rather sit by Jack than Andrew. This shows us clearly that Tilly can demonstrate her personal preferences included in the 'Me, Myself and I' Component.

- At 12:10pm we can see that Tilly has clearly expressed her preference to sleep in her pushchair, but Sue has offered her recognition of this fact, ensuring that she feels accepted and comforted at sleep time. This is expanded in 'Being Acknowledged and Affirmed'.

- At 11:30am Tilly confidently manages to eat most of her lunch before taking up Sue's offer of help. Here she is demonstrating that she is clearly becoming confident in what she can do and is developing self-assurance.

- At 2:30pm Tilly is comfortable in joining in with another group at story time. She clearly demonstrates a sense of belonging to this extended group.

Once you are comfortable with your inclusions for 'A Strong Child', move on to 'A Skilful Communicator', then to 'A Competent Learner' and finally 'A Healthy Child' for this exercise:

	Activity	Tick when completed
☞	This time, read through and find the two time slots that typify each of these Aspects and put a big circle around them.	

Take another look at 'A day in the life of Tilly Mint'. Can you still see areas that overlap? If you can, this means that you are seeing the wider picture and looking at Tilly's development as a whole. This, of course, is nothing to worry about and reflects our overall developmental progress, but as a further, optional exercise try to identify areas of her day with the Aspect that comes closest to it. To do this throughout the day would be very time-consuming and not at all practical, but it is helpful for you to know that you can do it!

Sample activity pages

Take a look at the first sample activity page (on page 57) in the 'Strong Child' section. This will help you use the activity pages in isolation (from the manual and the framework) and ensure that you have *all* of the key information to hand on just one piece of paper. You should recognise these headings:

- Aspect title.
- Component title.
- Development matters.
- Play and practical support.
- Note.

What you will not be familiar with are the elements relating to the activity itself:

- Sample activity.
- Resources.
- Health and safety.
- Layout.
- Role of the key worker.
- Questions.
- Comments.

The sample activity is a means of reminding ourselves about the type of activity that might address the issues identified in the Component pages. They also serve as a really good reminder for those times when we feel that we need a little refresher when drawing up our plans.

In order to guide your session, as much information as possible has been included while at the same time keeping it manageable. For example, in our 'Recognising me' activity (page 57), we see this list in the 'Resources' section:

- Child-safe mirrors;
- Reflective surfaces;
- A key worker with time for fun and quiet reflection.

We state these obvious facts to ensure that even the most inexperienced worker needs to remember that the mirrors selected must be child-safe and that this is a fun activity! We repeat the importance of this fact again in our 'Health and safety' section:

- Ensure that mirrors selected are appropriate for the age group and that freestanding mirrors are properly supported.

We do this again assuming that our activity may be carried out by the most novice practitioner and do not leave room for them to misinterpret our intentions.

In the 'Layout' section we give the practitioner more information about how we had seen our activity being carried out. Of course, you can be very specific when drawing up your own plans, listing your own equipment in your specific location.

The 'Role of the keyworker' section is, perhaps, the most important in ensuring that the activity is carried out as intended. Without careful thought given to the completion of this section, the activity may bear no relation to the one that you had planned. Here we provide this information for the key worker:

- Sit quietly at the child's level and observe. Watch how they use things near to them and where their gaze strays to. Talk with them about what they see and about what they are doing. Encourage them to look at the mirrors in different ways, perhaps using the mirrors to direct the gaze of babies. Share the mirrors with them, encouraging them to look at their own face as well as your own or those of other children. Change the mirrors for different types intermittently, allowing exploration without allowing the child to become bored with the same activity. Use the mirrors to reinforce positive self-image even in very young babies, describing beautiful brown eyes or lovely curly hair, for example.

In one paragraph we are giving a practitioner a real insight into the activity, helping to ensure that this activity really *does* support the areas identified in 'A Strong Child: Me, Myself and I'. Without this valuable information the practitioner may simply sit and let the baby play unsupported. What a different activity that would be!

To further reinforce the information provided in the framework, the 'Note' section is often taken directly from it. In 'Recognising Me' the practitioner is asked to:

- Note how babies use the opportunities you provide, to develop, show and communicate their preferences and decisions.

It is intended that practitioners use these notes as prompts for taking notes to add to each childs developmental files. When writing up your own activity planner you may prefer to note down a very specific request for a specific child or group of children.

To further support the 'Role of the key worker' section there are questions to ask. Only one or two ideas are suggested, but the intention is to highlight the fact that he/she *should* be asking questions of their children, whatever their age. I am sure we have all witnessed nursery staff setting out an activity and then taking a back seat while the children play. Prompting practitioners to ask questions reminds them that their job is not finished once the equipment is set up, but often, more importantly, offers another link between the activity and the Aspect/Component it is intended to address.

The questions 'Who can you see in the mirror?', 'Where's James?' and 'Where's James's nose?' are intended to set James thinking about who he can actually see and also what specifically he is looking at.

Next is a 'Comments' box. Throughout the manual this has been used for two different types of comment. In this example it has been completed as if the box had been left blank at the start of the activity and the practitioner had updated it with the following information:

- This was a very relaxing and enjoyable session that would definitely benefit from repeat sessions. More could have been achieved with a larger variety of mirrors, so will borrow more mirrors from other rooms for the next session.

This comment is very helpful to the next practitioner carrying out this activity and, of course, serves as a very valuable tool for demonstrating that we evaluate our sessions as a matter of course.

There are occasions where the 'Comments' box is used to serve as a reminder to the practitioner about certain matters. In the 'Peek-a-boo' activity (page 59), the comment reads:

- Try to play this right the way across the room to encourage a feeling of security that does not rely on proximity.

When drawing up your own activity planners you must decide which is appropriate for each planner, but remember to make a note of evaluative comments on the additional page so that other practitioners will benefit from your thoughts and, of course, that further sessions can take your thoughts into consideration before beginning.

Drawing up your own activity planner

If you are working through this section as part of a team meeting you might like to split up into groups for this next activity. It is recommended that you all choose the same activity to draw up though, as this will serve to highlight the differences and, of course, the importance of noting down exactly what you had intended from the very beginning.

	Activity	Tick when completed
☞	At the back of each section you will find a blank activity planner. Start by photocopying this for you to practise on.	
☞	Because we need to make a start somewhere, go to your planner for next week and choose the activity scheduled for Monday morning.	
☞	Starting at the 'Activity' row, take your time and complete the form up to and including the 'Questions to ask' box.	
☞	Once completed, take a good look at the activity you have drawn up and then spend some time thinking about where this activity would best fit into the framework. When you are happy with this, move on to complete the Aspect title.	
☞	Look at it further before completing the Component title as occasionally the most obvious is not the most appropriate.	
☞	Once you have done this go to the appropriate page in this manual that outlines the Component in more detail. Highlight the 'Development matters' section and enter this into your table exactly as it is written. Remember that these sheets may be used in isolation from the framework and/or this manual so we need to have all of the important information with us.	
☞	Before you enter the 'Play and practical support' section into your table, consider any amendments that you might like to make to suit your setting. Do this now.	
☞	Finally, look once more at your completed table. Would your activity benefit from additional notes in the 'Comments' section? Remember that leaving this section blank is perfectly acceptable, but only *if* there are no additional comments for you to make.	
☞	If you have split into several groups for this activity you should feed back to each other now. It is important that everybody is comfortable before moving on to the next exercise.	

Hopefully you can now see why we started with this activity. Being able to complete the table for activities that we already have planned will be helpful when it is time to implement this new planning system. Before long, though, you will need to plan from scratch, so then would be a good time to plan from a different perspective.

Let us take some time now to plan directly for Aspects and Components, and identify activities that support their requirements.

	Activity	Tick when completed
☞	Return to the same groups, but this time select different areas to plan for. If you have four groups you could suggest that you select activities as follows:	
	Group One ⟶ A Strong Child ⟶ Being Acknowledged and Affirmed	
	Group Two ⟶ A Skilful Communicator ⟶ Finding a Voice	
	Group Three ⟶ A Competent Learner ⟶ Being Imaginative	
	Group Four ⟶ A Healthy Child ⟶ Growing and Developing	
	This time start by completing the table from the top down, referring to the Components pages for confirmation of the requirements for the activity.	

	Activity	Tick when completed
☞	Now feed back to each other. Remember that each group needs to *inform* the others about exactly how and why the activity meets the requirements of the Components.	

Remember at this stage to remind everybody to be open to questioning. We all need to be comfortable that we understand what we are doing before we move on to the next section. Take some time to see each of the activities planned with a child in mind from that age group. Does it fit? Are there alterations to be made now that you can see a specific child in the activity? Are there alterations to be made if you give the planner to a certain practitioner? Will your descriptions need to be clearer, or the health and safety section more prescriptive? Of course, only you decide that, but remember to ask yourself those questions regularly.

There is one more exercise before we can discuss fitting our activity planners into our schedule. Think about an activity such as sand play. Of course, playing in the sand is 'Being Creative', isn't it? Or is it 'Being Imaginative'? Perhaps it is 'Finding a Voice' or 'Developing Self-assurance'? Well actually it could be all of these things. The key here is to identify clearly the Component that you are working towards and make sure that your 'Role of the key worker' and 'Questions' are addressed accordingly.

	Activity	Tick when completed
☞	For the final exercise in this section return to the same groups and select a different Aspect and Component completely at random and ask the groups to plan a sand activity that fits. Take only 5 minutes for this exercise as it is the realisation that we can do this that is the point, rather than the plans themselves that matter.	

Although sometimes we might identify just one small aspect of the play that is relevant, we can make sand play fit into *any* of the Components listed. Imagine how useful this is for a child who is only comfortable at one or two activities and needs a little support to become comfortable with different situations. In future meetings you might want to review this and choose a different activity to fit into each of the Components.

Using the framework to support your teams

Looking closely at our 'Day in the life of Tilly Mint' you will see how often the unplanned parts of Tilly's day can be included when assessing her development. We saw Components covered as she arrived in the morning and went home at the end of the day. More are addressed at meal times, nappy changes and even putting on coats to go out to play. Of course, we know that these things count as areas of development, but how often do we remember to record them?

	Activity	Tick when completed
☞	Take some time to look through her day and with a yellow highlighter go over unplanned events that can be recorded in Tilly's Tracker (or developmental chart).	

By doing this you will have drawn up a list of activities or events that are covered by the framework but that need no, or very little, planning on your part. You will, of course, need to remember to record them and remind all practitioners that these events are important.

Once this is completed you will then have a long list of areas that are not likely to be covered unless you include them in your plans. This will probably include art and craft activities, music, story times and physical challenges among others.

Take another look at your planner for next week. It may look a little like this:

Monday	Tuesday	Wednesday	Thursday	Friday
Shredded paper play	Gloop	Baby assault course challenge	Washing ourselves	Push-along toys
Making music from everyday objects	Recognising me	A tactile collage	Taste tests	A very messy painting activity

It certainly looks very interesting. Making a mess is great fun if it is for a purpose. In order to make this a more purposeful planner, what we need are some *outcomes*. Using a baby room as an example, we have 12 babies under 18 months, cared for by four practitioners. Of course, these babies do not fall easily into equal divisions according to the framework, so we need to plan our activities to suit the children expected for each individual session. Each key worker can identify the outcomes she has planned for her group of children. For example, Sue's planner might look like this when she has clearly identified her planned outcomes:

Monday	Tuesday	Wednesday	Thursday	Friday
Shredded paper play **SIT3**	Gloop **SIT12**	Baby assault course challenge **SIT15**	Washing ourselves **SIT4**	Push-along toys **SIT1**
Making music from everyday objects **SIT6**	Recognising me **SIT1**	A tactile collage **SIT11**	Taste tests **SIT16**	A very messy painting activity **SIT10**

Sue has planned for the following learning objectives:

SIT1	Me, Myself and I	**SIT3**	Developing Self-assurance
SIT4	A Sense of Belonging	**SIT6**	Finding a voice
SIT10	Being Imaginative	**SIT11**	Being Creative
SIT12	Representing	**SIT15**	Keeping Safe
SIT16	Healthy Choices		

Sue will know the abilities of her group and will be conversant with the Trackers (developmental progress records) for each of her children, and will work towards reinforcing areas from these Components where her support is needed.

Later on in the year, as the children in her group have developed, we might see the same planner adapted to take this into account:

Monday	Tuesday	Wednesday	Thursday	Friday
Shredded paper play **SIT5**	Gloop **SIT9**	Baby assault course challenge **SIT15**	Washing ourselves **SIT3**	Push-along toys **SIT15**
Making music from everyday objects **SIT11**	Recognising me **SIT1**	A tactile collage **SIT11**	Taste tests **SIT3**	A very messy painting activity **SIT10**

The list of learning objectives now looks like this:

SIT1	Me, Myself and I	**SIT3**	Developing Self-assurance
SIT5	Being Together	**SIT9**	Making Connections
SIT10	Being Imaginative	**SIT11**	Being Creative
SIT13	Emotional Well-being	**SIT15**	Keeping Safe

We can see that several of the same objectives are included to ensure that all aspects of the Component are covered, but here we can see several new Components listed. This could be for several reasons. Firstly, Sue will have identified that individuals in her group may be ready to move on to a further challenge and she plans for this accordingly. Secondly, it is unlikely that we can *plan* every Component for inclusion each week without giving us a very boring planner. We are *likely* to cover each of the Components each week through a mixture of planned and spontaneous activities so there is no need to take any further action here.

Use a similar grid on a large piece of paper to record your unplanned events. Every now and again, when you see a Component covered spontaneously, note down the appropriate code with the child's name on a Post-it note. Stick this on to the grid for later recording. For Tilly Mint you might see the following Components recorded:

Monday	Tuesday	Wednesday	Thursday	Friday
Peek-a-boo **SIT2**	Welcome to nursery **SIT13**	Can you find ...? **SIT5**	Making choices at snack time **SIT8**	What happens if you watch me paint? **SIT10**
Cardboard box play **SIT9**	Making music from everyday objects **SIT6**	Getting ready for a nap **SIT14**	Whose coat is this? **SIT1**	What's in this box? **SIT3**

Using the activity planners for the first time

Look again at your planner for next week. You will probably have at least ten core activities listed, possibly more. Don't panic. It is unlikely that you will have time to plan each of these activities now, but stop and think. We have already made a start on some of these activities in our earlier exercises and as long as you are happy with the results you can start using them straight away.

Having completed these exercises in your training session you should feel comfortable completing the activity planners as you go along and it is recommended that you try to have two written up each day. It will take a few weeks to cover all of your main activities, but also during this time try to encourage your team to write up one or two spontaneous events each week. Of course, you can take turns with other members of the team so that the task does not become too much of a chore, but consider how much more confident individuals will feel in an Ofsted inspection when they can demonstrate their detailed plans to an inspector *and* the recording of spontaneous activities as well!

Monitoring your progress

It is important to remind ourselves that the completion of the activity sheet is not the end product. Each time the activity has been carried out the practitioner will need to add dated comments to the second sheet to inform others of their findings. You can, of course, copy as many of these as you may need to ensure that evaluation and assessment is working to your advantage. By monitoring activities as we go along we are demonstrating a commitment to keeping our plans up to date and using the most recent assessments to the benefit of the children in our care.

Let us look once more at Tilly Mint. We have built up a picture of a Strong Child, a Skilful Communicator, a Competent Learner *and* a Healthy Child – yet Tilly is just 14 months old. She is another four months away from becoming a Mover, Shaker and Player. What are we to do to ensure that Tilly continues to develop into a confident and competent child? For Tilly it will be important that we watch her progress closely for a short period of time. Pay special attention to any gaps identified and watch for any areas that are identified strengths or weaknesses. Imagine, for example, that Tilly was such a Strong Child that she really needed more additional challenges in this area to prevent her becoming bored and frustrated. All we need to do is look for the purple pages in the next section and move on. There is no need to be bound by age restrictions. The ages are there simply because in most cases they are appropriate. In some they are not. Remember that this can work both ways and it may also be helpful with some children to look to pages in earlier sections for support.

Over a period of a few weeks you will be able to see a picture developing of some familiar Components reoccurring regularly throughout your planners. What you may not spot easily are those Components that are regularly overlooked. You will need to develop your own system to help you spot these, but one of the most efficient ways of identifying gaps in your planning is to complete a regular 'A day in the life of …' for the children in your group, as demonstrated with Tilly Mint. If each of your key workers takes more detailed notes for just one day each week and writes/types them up in a similar fashion to Tilly's day, you can demonstrate that not only are you assessing your practice overall, but you are also assessing it more closely in relation to individual children. An added bonus is that your parents will love this detailed record of their child's day, which of course can be adjusted to suit your own needs. If you have somebody with good IT skills you could include digital photographs in your table, showing the child painting, sleeping, eating etc. Save each of these in a loose-leaf file and before long you will have a fantastic record of evidence for use in Ofsted inspections, parents evenings, open days or any other opportunity to show off the children's progress.

Summary

By the time you have completed all of the exercises in this book and worked with the system for a month or so you will be able to:

- identify and plan for each of your under three age groups according to the *Birth to three matters* framework;

- draw up specific activity planners to guide and support the practitioners in your team;

- make additional comments each time the activity is carried out to keep other practitioners informed;

- record spontaneous events in a similar format;

- evaluate your planning;

- further identify gaps to be addressed in your children's development by transferring observations made to developmental Trackers*.

And finally …

To make this manual a *real* success for your under threes team it will be important to remember that this should be a working document. Make comments about questions raised, lessons learned or even nightmare activities that should *never* be repeated unless we take a number of precautions first.

---

*The Trackers referred to here are those published by QEd Publications (contact details at the front of the book). There are two books in the series – *Trackers 0–3* and *Trackers 3–5*, both simple and effective in monitoring the progress that children make between 0 to 3 years and 3 to 5 years.

Heads Up, Lookers
and
Communicators

(0–8 months)

Heads Up, Lookers and Communicators
(0–8 months)

Section index

Notes for this section

Practitioners inexperienced with this age group often incorrectly assume that there are not many activities worth planning; the common misconception being that babies in this group eat, sleep, cry and need their nappies changed. The *Birth to three matters* framework reminds us categorically that this is not so. Establishing two-way conversation, for example, is vital to a young baby's development, and with this age group conversation can be lots of fun.

Hopefully, many of the sample activities included here will provide food for thought for both new and experienced practitioners. Remember, though, that whichever activity you are planning, it needs to be suitable to the age and stage of development of the young babies involved. Quite a big ability gap is evident between the ages of nought and eight months, so look carefully at your children before including these plans in your schedule.

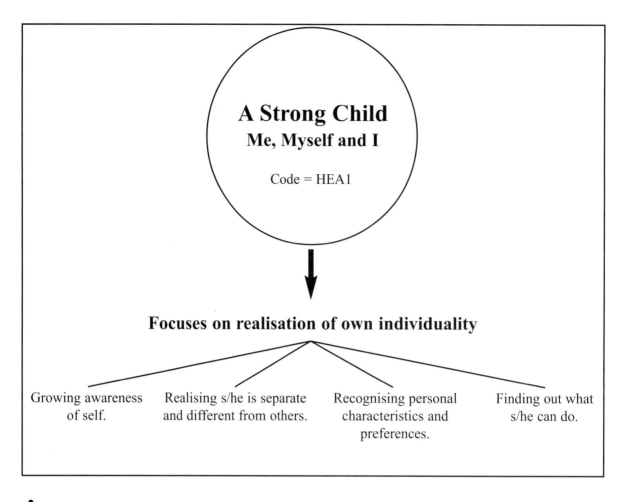

A Strong Child

Me, Myself and I

Code = HEA1

Focuses on realisation of own individuality

| Growing awareness of self. | Realising s/he is separate and different from others. | Recognising personal characteristics and preferences. | Finding out what s/he can do. |

Development matters

Young babies become aware of themselves as separate from others, learning also that they have influence upon and are influenced by others.

Look, listen, note

Note how young babies begin to explore their bodies' movements and the environment in individual ways.

Effective practice

Adults who respond to and build on babies' actions, expressions and gestures.

Play and practical support

Playfully imitate young babies, giving full eye contact, interacting with them and their playthings, watching the ways they use them and showing them new things to do.

Heads Up, Lookers and Communicators

A Strong Child
Me, Myself and I

Development matters	Play and practical support
Young babies become aware of themselves as they separate from others, learning also that they have influence *upon* and are influenced *by* others.	Playfully imitate young babies, giving them full eye contact, interacting with their playthings, watching the ways they use them and showing them new things to do.

Sample activity	Toys with movement.
Resources	Gather together a selection of toys that make movement but don't move away – spinning tops, dancing teddies etc.
Health and safety	Ensure that the baby does not topple forward onto a toy that may hurt her.
Layout	Sit the young baby carefully propped up with lots of soft cushions so that she can move safely. Arrange a selection of the toys within sight of the young baby and sit facing her.
The role of the key worker	Take your lead from the young baby's gaze and watch how she reacts when you set one of the toys off. Encourage her to help set it off again, using her own hand to push the top down. Maintaining full eye contact keep her interest by encouraging participation, moving on to the next toy as her attention decreases. Return to favourite toys intermittently, aiming to extend her interaction with the toy.
Note	Note how young babies begin to explore their body's movements and the environment in individual ways.
Questions to ask/ suggested interactions	• Can you reach this spinning top? • Can you push your hand down to make it go again? • Shall we try another toy? • Which one would you like?
Comments	Make notes of her favourite toys and those that don't go down too well. Also note where progress is made with extended reach or imitating your actions to set the toy off.

Heads Up, Lookers and Communicators

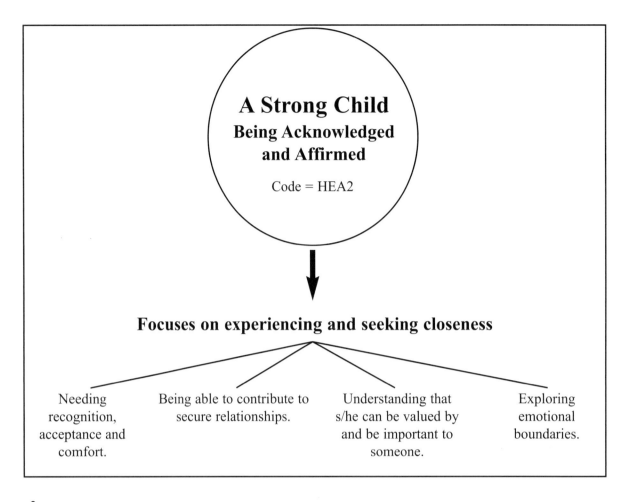

A Strong Child
Being Acknowledged
and Affirmed

Code = HEA2

Focuses on experiencing and seeking closeness

Needing recognition, acceptance and comfort.

Being able to contribute to secure relationships.

Understanding that s/he can be valued by and be important to someone.

Exploring emotional boundaries.

Development matters	Young babies seek to be looked at, approved of and find comfort in touch and in the human face.
Look, listen, note	Observe how young babies respond to your attention, noting whether they make eye contact or vocalise.
Effective practice	Be aware of the importance of your facial expressions and body language.
Play and practical support	Find time to play, have fun, sing and laugh with young babies.

Heads Up, Lookers and Communicators

A Strong Child

Being Acknowledged and Affirmed

Code = HEA2

Development matters	Play and practical support
Young babies seek to be looked at, approved of and find comfort in touch and in the human face.	Find time to play, have fun, sing and laugh with young babies.

Sample activity	Let's all join in with nursery rhymes!
Resources	No resources required at all … unless you want to extend your range of nursery rhymes and sing along with a children's CD.
Health and safety	There are no health and safety risks to this activity.
Layout	Sit or lie all of the children in a circle in a comfortable position.
The role of the key worker	Sitting at the same level as the young babies, maintain a contact with one or two of the group throughout, making sure that there are enough staff to incorporate all of the group meaningfully. Select a small repertoire of songs with a tactile feel, perhaps starting with a song that welcomes everybody into the session. 'Hello, Holly Richardson, and how are you?', repeated for each of the participating young babies and shaking each of their hands as you sing their name offers great opportunities for eye-to-eye contact, physical contact and name recognition. Moving on to different songs, the key worker can move the young baby's hands to touch her head, shoulders, knees and toes, building up the fun element as the speed increases. Other movement songs such as 'Wind my bobbin up' allow for similar fun.
Note	Remember to agree on tunes beforehand if more than one exists for a particular song. Select a small number of songs to sing regularly, returning to the same ones often. Introduce new ones sparingly, but intermingled with old favourites.
Questions to ask/ suggested interactions	• Did you enjoy that one, Holly? • Shall we sing 'Wheels on the bus' now? • Can Holly clap her hands?
Comments	Remember to include all of the young babies in the introductory session, repeating it if others arrive to join your group. Try not to use too many different songs over a short period, but do try to make your selection varied.

Heads Up, Lookers and Communicators

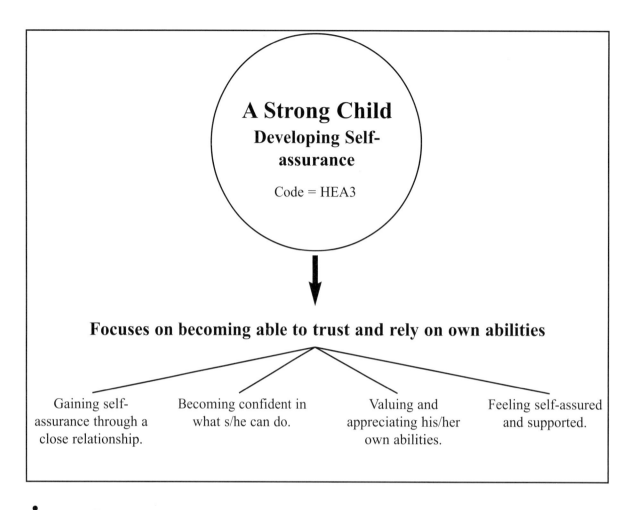

A Strong Child
Developing Self-assurance

Code = HEA3

↓

Focuses on becoming able to trust and rely on own abilities

| Gaining self-assurance through a close relationship. | Becoming confident in what s/he can do. | Valuing and appreciating his/her own abilities. | Feeling self-assured and supported. |

Development matters

Young babies enjoy the company of others, and also need to feel safe and loved when they are not the centre of adult attention.

Look, listen, note

Observe and note the length of time young babies occupy themselves and whether this depends on the time of day.

Effective practice

Provide support for babies when they are not with their key person to give them manageable experiences of being with others.

Play and practical support

Give young babies a favourite or preferred toy and encourage them to play independently under your watchful eye.

Heads Up, Lookers and Communicators

A Strong Child
Developing Self-assurance

Code = HEA3

Development matters	Play and practical support
Young babies enjoy the company of others and also need to feel safe and loved when they are not the centre of adult attention.	Give young babies a favourite or preferred toy and encourage them to play independently under your watchful eye.

Sample activity	Shredded paper play.
Resources	A large bag of shredded paper from a recognised source to guarantee that it is clean and safe.
Health and safety	Ensure that the baby does not take too much paper into his mouth.
Layout	Prop the young baby in an inflated play ring so that he is comfortable. Place a few handfuls of the shredded paper into the play ring, across the young baby's lap.
The role of the key worker	Sit and play with the shredded paper with the young baby for a few minutes, encouraging him to feel the paper crinkling in his fingers. After making sure that he is comfortable, sit to one side so that he can still see you, but let him explore the feeling of the paper by himself. If the young baby makes attempts to involve you in the activity, do not ignore him, but talk to him from where you are in a cheerful way, to help him feel safe to continue playing on his own.
Note	The young baby might feel uncomfortable playing on his own, particularly if shredded paper is new to him. Try to start with an activity that you know he enjoys, but is not dependent on your participation to make it fun.
Questions to ask/ suggested interactions	• Can you clap your hands in the paper?
Comments	Remember that the important part of this activity is to encourage independent play. If the young baby appears to be comfortable on his own, keep a watchful eye, but do not interfere. Respond when he makes gabbling noises or when he looks over to you, but do not join in with his play unless you are ready to wrap up the session.

Heads Up, Lookers and Communicators

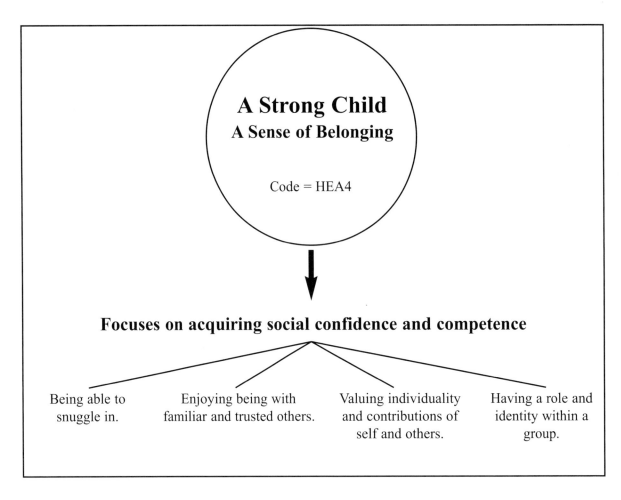

A Strong Child
A Sense of Belonging

Code = HEA4

Focuses on acquiring social confidence and competence

Being able to snuggle in.

Enjoying being with familiar and trusted others.

Valuing individuality and contributions of self and others.

Having a role and identity within a group.

Development matters	Snuggling in gives young babies physical, psychological and emotional comfort.
Look, listen, note	Note when you provide opportunities for young babies to snuggle in. Is it only when you have time or is it in response to their needs?
Effective practice	Recognise that young babies will find comfort from snuggling in with a variety of objects and people in different places, such as cosy corners with soft, inviting surfaces.
Play and practical support	Talk to parents about significant events in the young baby's day. Ask them about important evens at home and encourage them to contribute to their baby's records.

Heads Up, Lookers and Communicators

A Strong Child

A Sense of Belonging

Development matters	Play and practical support
Snuggling in gives young babies physical, psychological and emotional comfort.	Provide experiences that involve using all of the senses, such as relaxing music, soft lighting and pleasant smells for the babies to enjoy.

Sample activity	A sensory session to relax and feel warm and secure.
Resources	If you have a sensory room you could select one calming light effect and calming music. A lamp projecting colourful images would be useful, but not necessary. Select a calming music-based CD rather than a sing-along tape. High on a shelf put out some calming lavender or peppermint oil.
Health and safety	Ensure that any scented oils are placed securely out of the babies' reach.
Layout	Lay out plenty of floor cushions and dim the lights to show your colourful images to their best. Use a coloured bulb in an ordinary lamp if you do not have access to any light effects. Play the music quietly so that you can still hear young babies vocalising.
The role of the key worker	If possible select a time when you can give your attention to just one young baby. Lie next to them or sit facing them so that they can maintain eye contact with you. Talk soothingly to the baby, using baby massage techniques to make them aware of relaxing their arms, legs, hands etc. Talk gently through what you are doing and ensure that as much close eye contact is achieved as the young baby is comfortable with.
Note	Note when you provide opportunities for young babies to snuggle in. Is it only when you have time or is it in response to their needs? Try to avoid using it just at times when you are encouraging young babies to go to sleep.
Questions to ask/ suggested interactions	• Talk gently to the baby throughout this session. • Describe light and sound effects where relevant.
Comments	Before beginning this session try to discourage other staff from interrupting to borrow toys etc. Remember that many things arising in this session may also be included in 'A Healthy Child – Emotional Well-being'. Talk to parents about significant events in the young baby's day. Ask them about important events at home and encourage them to contribute to their babies' records.

Heads Up, Lookers and Communicators

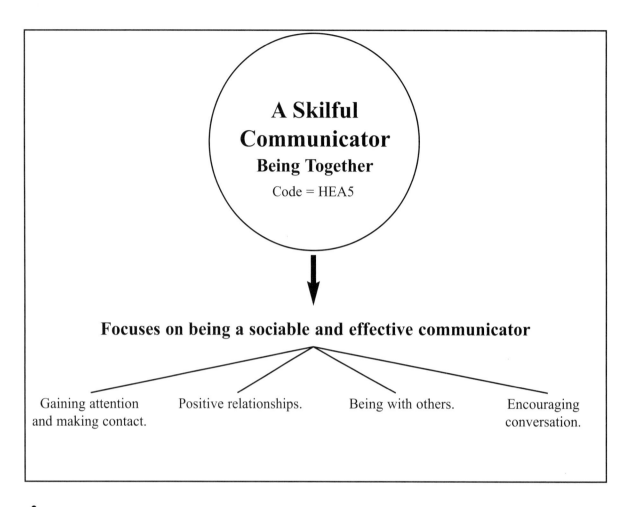

A Skilful Communicator

Being Together

Code = HEA5

Focuses on being a sociable and effective communicator

Gaining attention and making contact.

Positive relationships.

Being with others.

Encouraging conversation.

Development matters	Young babies are sociable from birth, using a variety of ways to gain attention.
Look, listen, note	Note the skills babies use to make contact, e.g. inclining their heads, wiggling their toes, eye contact, banging, smiling, vocalising.
Effective practice	Being physically close and making eye contact, using touch or voice provides an ideal opportunity for early conversations between adults and babies; and one baby and another.
Play and practical support	Mobiles above changing areas, feathers to tickle and music to share, help young babies to enjoy being together and communicating with their key person.

Heads Up, Lookers and Communicators

A Skilful Communicator
Being Together

Code = HEA5

Development matters	Play and practical support
Young babies are sociable from birth, using a variety of ways to gain attention.	Mobiles above changing areas, feathers to tickle and music to share, help young babies to enjoy being together and communicating with their key person.

Sample activity	Using the baby gym for a shared activity.
Resources	A safe and secure baby gym, interchangeable pennants to hang from it.
Health and safety	Ensure that the pennants selected are appropriate for your child's age group and that they cannot come detached from the gym causing harm to the baby.
Layout	Make the young baby comfortable underneath a baby gym with one or two pennants already selected for use.
The role of the key worker	Sit close to one side and observe the young baby. Watch how she focuses on the pennants hanging from the gym, and then how she attempts to make contact with you. Responding to her communications positively should encourage more or different communications with you, taking the form of a conversation without words. Remember to maintain eye contact and change the pennants as the baby tires of them.
Note	Note the skills the young baby uses to make contact, e.g. inclining her head, wiggling her toes, making eye contact, banging hands/feet/objects, smiling and vocalising.
Questions to ask/ suggested interactions	• What can we see hanging here? • Can you feel the feathers tickling your hands and feet? • Do you like it when I do this?
Comments	Remember to vary the pennants hanging from the gym, the gym itself and, of course, the young baby's position; they could be lying flat for one session, half-raised the next time and propped quite upright for another. Plan each session to the changing skill level of the young baby involved.

Heads Up, Lookers and Communicators

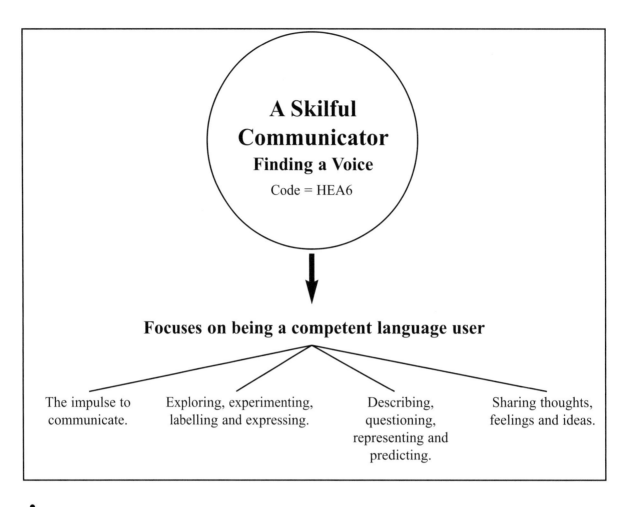

A Skilful Communicator
Finding a Voice
Code = HEA6

Focuses on being a competent language user

| The impulse to communicate. | Exploring, experimenting, labelling and expressing. | Describing, questioning, representing and predicting. | Sharing thoughts, feelings and ideas. |

Development matters

Young babies communicate in a variety of ways including crying, gurgling, babbling and squealing.

Look, listen, note

Note the wide variety of sounds a young baby produces and how adults try to understand and respond to them.

Effective practice

Adults interpret, give meaning to and echo young babies who are making a variety of sounds.

Play and practical support

Use everyday routines such as dressing, changing and mealtimes to sing with, talk to and encourage babies to vocalise.

Heads Up, Lookers and Communicators

A Skilful Communicator
Finding a Voice

Development matters	Play and practical support
Young babies communicate in a variety of ways including crying, gurgling, babbling and squealing.	Use everyday routines such as dressing, changing and mealtimes to sing with, talk to and encourage babies to vocalise.

Sample activity	Experimenting with our voice.
Resources	Large pictures or models from our selected subject matter, e.g. farmyard animals.
Health and safety	There are no health and safety risks to this activity.
Layout	Sit comfortably facing your young baby or group of babies and ensure that the babies are comfortable with a clear view of your face.
The role of the key worker	Choose a simple story with colourful supporting images such as *On the Farm* (published by Usborne) and read the story to your group. Using varying tones of voice, keep an interesting facial expression and eye contact with your group. Point out the farmyard animals in the picture and make the sounds associated with that animal. Encourage the young babies to join in, praising communication throughout. Remember to keep them fun and interesting, using the storybook as a loose outline for your story. Repeat phrases that have been well received and remember to include key phrases that the family might say for the baby to repeat also.
Note	Note the wide variety of sounds a young baby produces and how adults try to understand and respond to them.
Questions to ask/ suggested interactions	• What does the cow say? The cow says 'Mooooo'. • What did the farmer say? The farmer says 'Morning!' • Shall we read that story again?
Comments	It is never too early to introduce babies to story time. The key to success is choosing a small selection of stories, repeating them regularly and making them sound exciting but familiar. This went down extremely well, with the young babies who were still interested after the second reading. Shame I didn't have more time to read it through again.

Heads Up, Lookers and Communicators

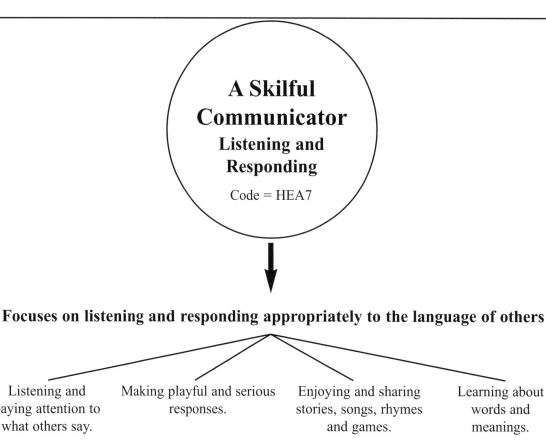

A Skilful Communicator
Listening and Responding

Code = HEA7

Focuses on listening and responding appropriately to the language of others

| Listening and paying attention to what others say. | Making playful and serious responses. | Enjoying and sharing stories, songs, rhymes and games. | Learning about words and meanings. |

Development matters

Long before young babies can communicate verbally, they listen to, distinguish and respond to intonations in adults' voices.

Look, listen, note

Note the ways in which the gestures and sounds of very young babies change when you respond to them.

Effective practice

Encourage playfulness, turn-taking and responses, including peek-a-boo and rhymes with young babies.

Play and practical support

Have fun with babies by making a game of everyday activities such as waiting for fingers to pop out of a sleeve, or head through a vest when dressing.

Heads Up, Lookers and Communicators

A Skilful Communicator
Listening and Responding

Development matters	Play and practical support
Long before young babies can communicate verbally, they listen to, distinguish and respond to intonations in adults' voices.	Have fun with babies by making a game of everyday activities, such as waiting for fingers to pop out of a sleeve, or head through a vest when dressing.

Sample activity	Peek-a-boo after an afternoon nap.
Resources	Gather together the clothes that you will dress the young baby in when they wake from their sleep.
Health and safety	There are no health and safety risks to this activity.
Layout	With the young baby ready to wake from her afternoon sleep make some space so that you can sit nearby and play comfortably with the clothes you will dress her in, and the sheets from her bed.
The role of the key worker	Wait until the young baby is awake and ready to play. Start with the sheets from her bed and hide behind it. Peek from behind it and make eye contact while laughing. Then hide the baby's face with the sheet, asking 'Where's Holly gone?' When putting on clothes gradually, remember to point out hands hidden in sleeves, her head popping through her vest etc.
Note	Note the ways in which the gestures and sounds of very young babies change when you respond to them.
Questions to ask/ suggested interactions	• Where's Holly gone? • Where's Holly's hand gone?
Comments	This is often a time when caregivers can be rushing to prepare for the next session or finish their list of nappy changes. Remember that every opportunity helps encourage the child to become a skilful communicator.

Heads Up, Lookers and Communicators

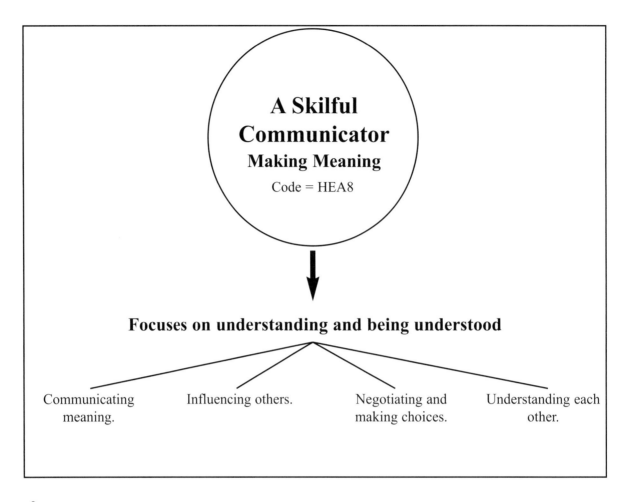

A Skilful Communicator
Making Meaning

Code = HEA8

Focuses on understanding and being understood

Communicating meaning.

Influencing others.

Negotiating and making choices.

Understanding each other.

Development matters	From the very beginning of life, young babies convey messages about what they want and need, as well as how they feel.
Look, listen, note	Note how young babies influence adult behaviour and the ways in which different adults respond.
Effective practice	Try to tune into the different messages young babies are attempting to convey. Share your interpretations with parents and other staff.
Play and practical support	Let young babies know you understand what they are saying, such as when they are hungry, tired, happy, sad and lonely.

Heads Up, Lookers and Communicators

A Skilful Communicator
Making Meaning

Code = HEA8

Development matters	Play and practical support
From the very beginning of life, young babies convey messages about what they want and need, as well as how they feel.	Let young babies know you understand what they are saying, such as when they are hungry, tired, happy, sad and lonely.

Sample activity	Lunchtime.
Resources	A comfortable chair, a bib, a bottle and/or lunch as required.
Health and safety	Ensure that all of the normal health and safety checks associated with lunchtime are in place.
Layout	If possible, sit yourself aside from distractions with the baby's meal requirements to hand.
The role of the key worker	Talk to the young baby throughout the session, starting with the settling in period while the bottle is being warmed or food cooled. If the baby is fractious, put words to their feelings: 'I know youre hungry, dinner won't be much longer.' Respond to the babies' communications throughout the session, whether they are verbal (crying or screaming) or physical (turning heads away or stiffening bodies). Whatever their mood, try to ensure a calm and soothing manner so that the young baby knows that you understand and that you are helping. If they turn their face away from the food, ask them: 'Have you had enough?' and perhaps offer a drink or next course.
Note	Note how young babies influence adult behaviour and the ways in which different adults respond.
Questions to ask/ suggested interactions	• Can you open your mouth for this little spoon? • Have you had enough? • Do you want something to drink?
Comments	Opportunities should be taken whenever possible to feed especially young babies with this approach. Of course, in a busy baby room it is not always possible. Similar opportunities may still be provided in a small group environment and this also adds different learning activities. Often young babies can be tired, hungry and uncomfortable all at the same time and we know that this often occurs just before a meal time. Try to time the babies' meal time to avoid this, but if this is not feasible use distractions and a calming manner to minimise their frustration.

Heads Up, Lookers and Communicators

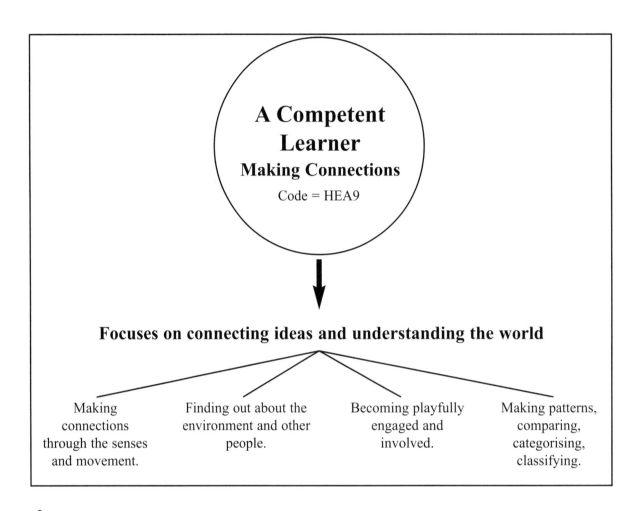

A Competent
Learner
Making Connections
Code = HEA9

Focuses on connecting ideas and understanding the world

Making connections through the senses and movement.

Finding out about the environment and other people.

Becoming playfully engaged and involved.

Making patterns, comparing, categorising, classifying.

Development matters

Young babies use movement and sensory exploration to connect with their immediate environment.

Look, listen, note

How young babies use their senses to investigate your hair, jewellery, own clothes.

Effective practice

Following young babies' lead as they explore their environment, people and resources.

Play and practical support

Use feeding, changing and bathing time to play with young babies, e.g. finger play, such as 'Round and round the garden'.

Heads Up, Lookers and Communicators

A Competent Learner
Making Connections

Code = HEA9

Development matters	Play and practical support
Young babies use movement and sensory exploration to connect with their immediate environment.	Use feeding, changing and bathing time to play with young babies, e.g. finger play such as 'Round and round the garden'.

Sample activity	Exploring the garden on a bright day.
Resources	A comfortable reclining chair that can be placed in different locations in the garden. Warm outdoor clothes that are not too restricting.
Health and safety	Take great care to ensure that hands and faces cannot be scratched by shrubs, and that you do not choose shrubs with dangerous berries or flowers.
Layout	Choose an interesting part of the nursery garden that has low-growing plants or shrubs of different textures and different types of movement.
The role of the key worker	Place the young baby (or group of babies) carefully among the plants so that the leaves blowing in the wind will blow across the young babies' laps and over their fingers. If you have a selection of different shaped leaved plants, move young babies to explore different textures, as well as feeling different shadows from the sun shining through the leaves. Ensure that scented flowers are included when available. Keep the session short in the colder months, but do not necessarily rule out this type of session if there is a light rain. Sensible dressing and short sessions are important considerations.
Note	Note how young babies use their senses to investigate your hair, jewellery, own clothes.
Questions to ask/ suggested interactions	• Can you hear the wind blowing through the trees? • Can you wriggle your fingers to make these leaves rustle?
Comments	If your own outdoor environment is not conducive to these activities, take a group of young babies for a walk in the park, parking the buggy for short periods near to different shrubs or flowers. In the summer young babies can be laid on a grassy area (after checking it for foreign bodies) to encourage them to feel the different textures of grass.

Heads Up, Lookers and Communicators

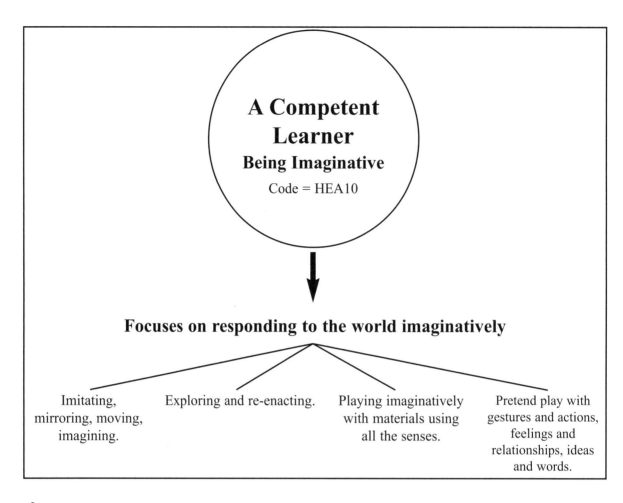

A Competent Learner

Being Imaginative

Code = HEA10

↓

Focuses on responding to the world imaginatively

Imitating, mirroring, moving, imagining.	Exploring and re-enacting.	Playing imaginatively with materials using all the senses.	Pretend play with gestures and actions, feelings and relationships, ideas and words.

Development matters — Young babies enjoy learning by imitating others.

Look, listen, note — Note the situations in which young babies mimic their key person's facial expressions, movements and sounds.

Effective practice — Playful interactions in which young babies and adults imitate and mimic each other.

Play and practical support — A playful adult is a valuable resource for a young baby. Even sticking out your tongue, wiggling your fingers and tickling is an important game for them.

Heads Up, Lookers and Communicators

A Competent Learner
Being Imaginative

Development matters	Play and practical support
Young babies enjoy learning by imitating others.	A playful adult is a valuable resource for a young baby. Even sticking out your tongue, wiggling your fingers and tickling is an important game for them.

Sample activity	Copycats.
Resources	Anything that is at hand, but the game is still very enjoyable with just a young baby and a playful adult.
Health and safety	There are no health and safety risks to this activity.
Layout	Wherever you happen to be, but with a good view of each other.
The role of the key worker	Catch the eye of a watching young baby and smile. If the young baby smiles back, change your facial expression and watch as the young baby responds. Return to a smile to confirm that the young baby is still willing to play. Include sad expressions, big belly laughs, wrinkling your nose, pulling out your tongue, even covering your face with your hands or a nearby blanket. Keep returning to that first smile until you feel that the young baby is losing interest before closing your session.
Note	Note the situations in which young babies mimic their key person's facial expressions, movements and sounds.
Questions to ask/ suggested interactions	• Can you stick your tongue out? • Can you wiggle your tongue about too?
Comments	This is obviously a game that children of all ages will enjoy, but remember to tailor your copycat images to the baby you are playing with. Complex expressions or stringing too many different actions together before returning to smile are likely to frustrate even the youngest baby.

Heads Up, Lookers and Communicators

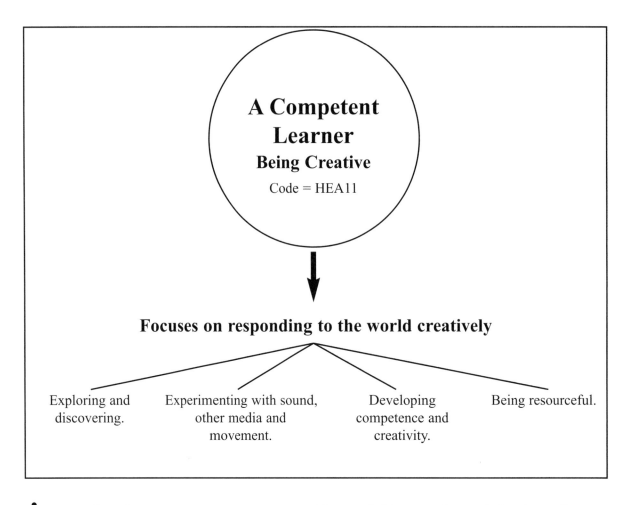

A Competent
Learner
Being Creative
Code = HEA11

Focuses on responding to the world creatively

Exploring and discovering.

Experimenting with sound, other media and movement.

Developing competence and creativity.

Being resourceful.

Development matters	Young babies explore their immediate environment of people, objects and feelings through all their senses.
Look, listen, note	Note the novel ways young babies find out more about themselves and their environment as they become mobile.
Effective practice	Encourage young babies to enjoy repetition in their movement, language, music and other sensory experiences.
Play and practical support	Use finger play, rhymes and familiar songs from home to support young babies' exploration and enjoyment in learning about their bodies and environment.

Heads Up, Lookers and Communicators

A Competent Learner
Being Creative

Development matters	Play and practical support
Young babies explore their immediate environment of people, objects and feelings through all of their senses.	Use finger play, rhymes and familiar songs from home to support young babies exploration and enjoyment in learning about their bodies and environment.

Sample activity	'This little piggy …'
Resources	None required.
Health and safety	There are no health and safety risks to this activity.
Layout	Start the session with a playful child (or even a young baby that needs distraction) and remove socks to expose bare toes.
The role of the key worker	Singing 'This little piggy went to market' take your time over each of the actions and gently wiggle or tickle the child's toes in turn. Repeat the rhyme with both feet, making sure that the experience is enjoyable and tactile throughout. After a while the young baby will learn to anticipate your actions, so prolonging each before moving on to the next will extend the young babies' enjoyment.
Note	Note the novel ways young babies find out more about themselves and their environment as they become more mobile.
Questions to ask/ suggested interactions	• Can you feel that tickling your little toes? • Shall we do that with the other foot?
Comments	The same fun and enjoyment can be shared with other tactile songs such as 'Tommy Thumb', 'Heads and shoulders, knees and toes' and in older babies 'Wind my bobbin up'.

Heads Up, Lookers and Communicators

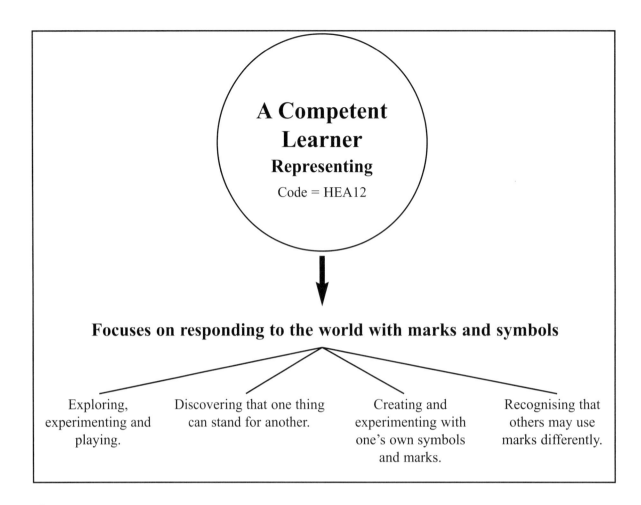

A Competent Learner

Representing

Code = HEA12

Focuses on responding to the world with marks and symbols

Exploring, experimenting and playing.

Discovering that one thing can stand for another.

Creating and experimenting with one's own symbols and marks.

Recognising that others may use marks differently.

Development matters

Young babies discover mark-making by chance, noticing, for instance, that fingers trailed through spilt juice can extend it.

Look, listen, note

Observe babies and children as they make marks in food, water, spilt drinks etc. How do they respond to what they have done? Do they repeat the action?

Effective practice

Talk to babies and children about the patterns and marks they make, showing them that you value what they do.

Play and practical support

Use gloop (corn flour and water) in small trays so babies and children can enjoy making marks on it.

Heads Up, Lookers and Communicators

A Competent Learner
Representing

Code = HEA12

Development matters	Play and practical support
Young babies discover mark-making by chance, noticing, for instance, that fingers trailed through spilt juice can extend it.	Use gloop (corn flour and water) in small trays so babies can enjoy making marks in it.

Sample activity	Gloop.
Resources	Cornflour, water, food colouring, shallow trays or the trays from the young baby's high chair, an apron to protect the child's clothing.
Health and safety	Ensure that the babies involved have no allergic tendencies towards any of the foodstuffs to be used. Watch closely and wipe hands occasionally if the babies are putting hands to mouths regularly.
Layout	Sit the young baby comfortably in his high chair, carefully covering his clothes with an apron, covering any carpet underfoot with a washable surface. If the surface/tray to be used is white, add a very small amount of food colouring to the gloop on preparation.
The role of the key worker	Sitting close to the young baby, place a small amount of the gloop into the tray and watch briefly for the young baby's reactions. If the young baby places his own fingers into the gloop and explores for himself, take a back seat and observe. If the young baby does not naturally explore the gloop himself, the key worker could either take the baby's hands gently and place them into the gloop, making trails with his fingers as an introduction, or put his own fingers into the gloop to see if the baby imitates his actions.
Note	Observe babies and children as they make marks in food, water, spilt drinks etc. How do they respond to what they have done? Do they repeat the action?
Questions to ask/ suggested interactions	• Does that feel funny on your fingers? • Can you make a pattern on your tray?
Comments	If the young baby enjoys this activity, on the next occasion include a different colour gloop. As the baby gets older and more used to it, two different colours might be used, placed at either ends of the tray to encourage the baby to watch as the colours merge, or are mixed by his fingers.

Heads Up, Lookers and Communicators

41

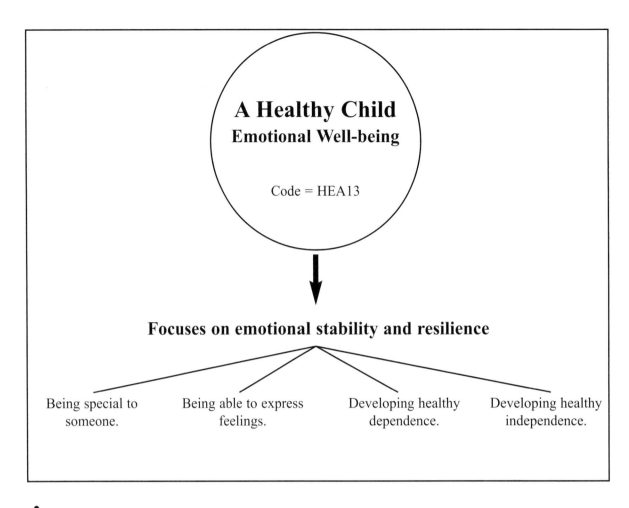

A Healthy Child
Emotional Well-being

Code = HEA13

Focuses on emotional stability and resilience

Being special to someone.

Being able to express feelings.

Developing healthy dependence.

Developing healthy independence.

Development matters

Young babies are social beings. They crave close attachments with a special person within their setting.

Look, listen, note

Observe and note the sounds and facial expressions young babies make in response to affectionate attention from their parent or their key person.

Effective practice

Key person and parent handing the young baby directly to each other at the beginning and end of each day.

Play and practical support

Introduce baby massage sessions to reduce stress and make young babies feel nurtured and valued.

Heads Up, Lookers and Communicators

A Healthy Child
Emotional Well-being

Code = HEA13

Development matters	Play and practical support
Young babies are social beings. They crave close attachments with a special person within their setting.	Introduce baby massage sessions to reduce stress and make young babies feel nurtured and valued.

Sample activity	Getting to know each other.
Resources	The young baby's key worker is all that is required. Calming music would be an added bonus.
Health and safety	There are no health and safety risks to this activity.
Layout	Make a space where the young baby can relax without too many distractions.
The role of the key worker	This session is about building strong relationships with the young babies in your key group. Make the child comfortable but ensure that there is a physical contact – perhaps sitting in the crook of your arm, lying on your lap etc. Talk to the young baby about the things that you are doing and include baby massage techniques to ensure she is enjoying the contact. Ensure that all young babies in your group are offered the same individual contact.
Note	Observe and note the sounds and facial expressions young babies make in response to affectionate attention from their parent or key person.
Questions to ask/ suggested interactions	• Ask the baby if they are enjoying you stroking their arms.
Comments	This activity is extremely personal to each of the young babies in your group, and careful notes should be made about elements that the young baby has enjoyed, but most particularly those that they have *not* enjoyed. It is important that a strong relationship is developed between the young babies and their key worker, but not to the exclusion of other workers in the group. Develop strategies among the team to deal with upset caused by staff absences.

Heads Up, Lookers and Communicators

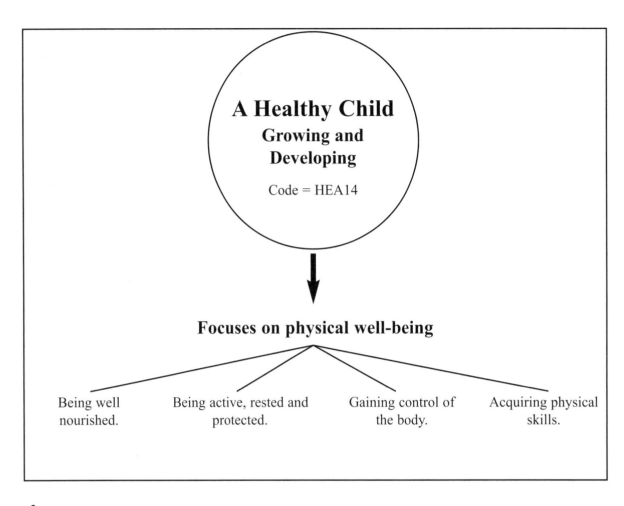

A Healthy Child
Growing and
Developing

Code = HEA14

Focuses on physical well-being

Being well nourished.

Being active, rested and protected.

Gaining control of the body.

Acquiring physical skills.

Development matters

Young babies thrive when both their nutritional and emotional needs are met.

Look, listen, note

Note young babies' hunger patterns and how they regulate the speed and intensity with which they suck.

Effective practice

Encourage and facilitate mothers breastfeeding their babies.

Play and practical support

Encourage the young baby to gradually share control of the bottle. This provides opportunities for sensory learning and increased independence.

Heads Up, Lookers and Communicators

A Healthy Child
Growing and Developing

Code = HEA14

Development matters	Play and practical support
Young babies thrive when both their nutritional and emotional needs are met.	Encourage the young baby to gradually share control of the bottle. This provides opportunities for sensory learning and increased independence.

Sample activity	Afternoon snack time.
Resources	Something tasty for the young baby to eat suitable for his age and stage of weaning development, and a bottle to drink from.
Health and safety	Ensure that all normal snack time health and safety checks are undertaken, remembering to double check for babies who are still not used to much solid food.
Layout	Seated in a social group with his peers so that he can feel part of the group.
The role of the key worker	Talking to the young babies in your group throughout this session is vital. Talk about the things that they are eating and how much they are enjoying it. Before the young baby is fully satisfied with his meal, put aside the bowl of food and exchange it with his bottle. Encourage the young baby to use one or two hands to help you hold his bottle, relinquishing your hold as the young baby becomes more experienced. Take care not to use this new found skill as a means of ignoring this particular young baby while you concentrate on others. Develop this skill as the baby moves on to finger foods to encourage a greater independence.
Note	Note young babies' hunger patterns and how they regulate the speed and intensity with which they suck.
Questions to ask/ suggested interactions	• Can you help me hold your bottle? • Clever boy! Can you hold it on your own?
Comments	It is easy to use a seated group time such as lunch or snack to chat with fellow workers, especially while young babies are busy eating. Remember that social chat among workers and children is an important part of our children's development, and young babies are no exception. Talk with your group of young babies about what they are eating, what will happen next or things that they can see around them.

Heads Up, Lookers and Communicators

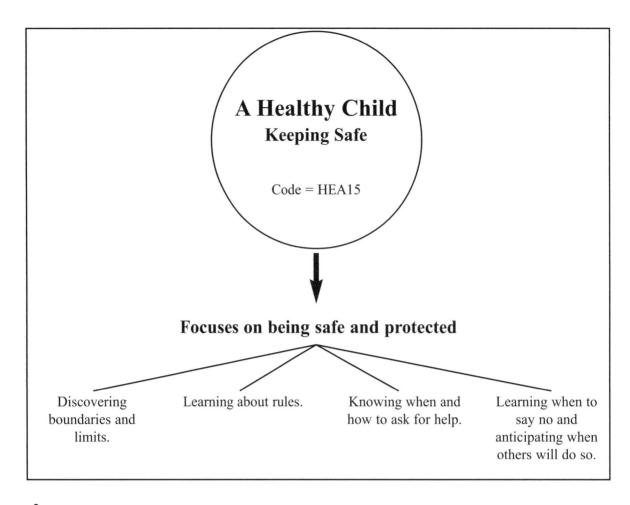

A Healthy Child
Keeping Safe

Code = HEA15

↓

Focuses on being safe and protected

Discovering boundaries and limits.

Learning about rules.

Knowing when and how to ask for help.

Learning when to say no and anticipating when others will do so.

Development matters	Young babies make strong and purposeful movements. They tend not to stay in the position in which they were placed.
Look, listen, note	Observe the ways in which young babies show determination in going for what they want.
Effective practice	Provide opportunities for babies and children to have choice in an environment kept safe by knowledgeable adults who know there should be a balance between freedom and safe limits.
Play and practical support	For young babies, provide different arrangements of toys and soft play materials to encourage crawling, hiding, peeping.

Heads Up, Lookers and Communicators

A Healthy Child
Keeping Safe

Development matters	Play and practical support
Young babies make strong and purposeful movements. They tend not to stay in the position in which they were placed.	For young babies, provide different arrangements of toys and soft play materials to encourage crawling, hiding and peeping.

Sample activity	Let's make some music.
Resources	A selection of freestanding musical instruments safe for this age group. Include rain makers, bells hanging from a small carousel, maracas and as many different sounding and attractive instruments as possible.
Health and safety	Ensure that babies do not inadvertently bash themselves or others during this activity.
Layout	Arrange the instruments in a semicircle around the head of a floor cushion onto which you are to lay the young baby.
The role of the key worker	Lay the young baby on her front with her head roughly central in the semicircle of instruments. Ensure that she can easily reach at least one of the collection and observe how she responds to it. Remember that there is no right or wrong way of making music with these instruments, but encourage her to bash, knock or shake the instruments to make interesting sounds. Watch as she moves her body, rolling to reach other instruments and rearrange the semicircle to ensure that she doesn't come to an empty space. Encourage her to use different methods of making sound, including banging loudly on the drum.
Note	Observe ways in which young babies show determination in going for what they want.
Questions to ask/ suggested interactions	• Can you shake your hands to make this maraca rattle? • Bash that drum as hard as you can.
Comments	Although this is a musical session, you can lay out the semicircle with any number of different toys. Try different teddies and soft toys with various textures, sounds and aspects. Remember not to overwhelm the young baby, and double check that she has not moved into the empty space deliberately before you fill it with something else.

Heads Up, Lookers and Communicators

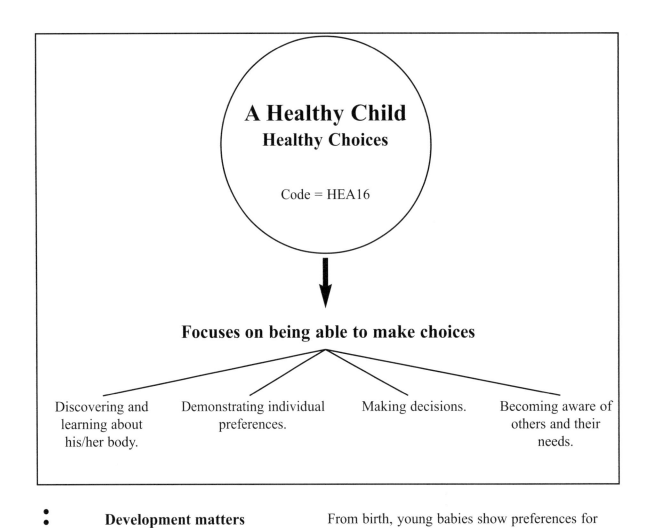

A Healthy Child
Healthy Choices

Code = HEA16

Focuses on being able to make choices

Discovering and learning about his/her body.

Demonstrating individual preferences.

Making decisions.

Becoming aware of others and their needs.

Development matters	From birth, young babies show preferences for people and for what they want to see, hear and taste.
Look, listen, note	Observe the strategies young babies use to demonstrate their likes and dislikes.
Effective practice	Provide opportunities for babies and children to make choices without overwhelming them.
Play and practical support	Allow time to observe what babies and children do when presented with several options.

Heads Up, Lookers and Communicators

A Healthy Child
Healthy Choices

Development matters	Play and practical support
From birth, young babies show preferences for people and for what they want to see, hear and taste.	Allow time to observe what babies and children do when presented with several options.

Sample activity	Take your pick …
Resources	A shelf or cupboard full of suitable toys.
Health and safety	Ensure that you are not offering babies toys that are not suitable for their age group.
Layout	Prepare a safe area for the young baby to play in after they have selected a toy.
The role of the key worker	Carry the young baby over to where you store a selection of toys that you know he is familiar with. Hold him in front of the selection and ask him to choose which toy he would like. At first this might prove impossible as making choices can be hard for all of us. After a while he will get used to this as an option and make it easier. Until he is familiar with it you could try several methods of encouraging selection. Try pointing and asking: 'Would you like to play with Elmo?' and watching to see how he responds. Often you will be in no doubt if the toy is a firm favourite, but if in doubt ask again: 'How about the laughing cow?' and again watch for reactions. Carry on until a toy is selected and place the young baby safely to play with his choice. Introduce this form of choice gradually – making sure that it is not too overwhelming a selection.
Note	Observe the strategies young babies use to demonstrate their likes and dislikes.
Questions to ask/ suggested interactions	• Would you like to play with this toy car? • Can you choose one of these toys to play with?
Comments	Make notes about his selections, but also about the toys he has declined. Try offering these toys amid a different selection where they may become the first choice. Remember that the young baby is not likely to want to play with his one choice for very long, so prepare a selection of toys similar to his selection.

Heads Up, Lookers and Communicators

Case study

A day in the life of Jamie Jones, aged five months

Time	Activity	Achieved
9:10	Jamie arrives at nursery with his mum who is running late for a meeting. Sensing the need for urgency, Jamie's key worker Rachel stops what she is doing and immediately goes over to help. She helps Mum take Jamie's coat and hat off, asking how he has been over the weekend. Taking Jamie from his mum, Rachel gives Jamie a big hug and encourages him to wave goodbye. The rest of the group are sitting down for a snack and although Jamie has had his breakfast at home, Rachel pulls up a high chair and sits him with the rest of the group. She gives him a small piece of rusk to chew on so that he doesn't feel left out.	HEA13 HEA8
9:30	As the snack is tidied away Rachel moves Jamie and a couple of other young babies to sit propped up by cushions and bouncer chairs in a small circle. She selects a CD and sits herself among the group. Singing along with the music she makes eye contact with the babies in her group in turn, taking their hands and encouraging them to join in.	HEA2 HEA4
10:00	Another child in Rachel's group becomes upset so she settles Jamie on a comfortable mat underneath a play gym and he happily kicks out to make the mobile pieces dance. After a while Jamie begins to laugh to himself and Sarah who is sitting nearby joins in and asks him what he is laughing at. He responds to her contact and struggles to turn himself more in Sarah's direction. Kicking faster in response he is happy to chat with Sarah from a distance now that he has a better view. Sarah deliberately moves out of Jamie's vision, quickly regaining eye contact saying 'Boo!' Jamie enjoys the game so Sarah continues for a little while until he is distracted and looks away.	HEA5 HEA7
10:30	Rachel has a painting session planned with some of her group, but Jamie will not be joining in today. Before starting painting she settles Jamie in his favourite inflatable play nest and fills the nest with light plastic balls from the ball pool. Jamie is happy to paddle his fingers around in the balls for quite some time, tasting some as he goes. Occasionally Rachel replaces balls that he has inadvertently thrown out.	HEA3
11:15	Nearly time for lunch so Rachel tidies away her painting activity and prepares to get Jamie's nappy changed. Talking to him while tidying away the last few pieces, he is waiting for her with arms and legs waving as she picks him up and takes him into the nappy change. Jamie needs a big clean-up before his new nappy goes on so Rachel talks to him constantly throughout. Tickling his tummy, his toes and chubby knees, Jamie is kept well entertained.	HEA13
11:45	Lunch is ready so Rachel spoon-feeds Jamie and Holly, talking to them throughout. Holly is more impatient for her lunch than Jamie, but Rachel responds to Jamie's smacking his lips for more with a laugh. After finishing lunch Jamie is ready for his bottle, so Rachel takes him out of his high chair and sits comfortably cuddling Jamie while he drinks from his bottle. Although he is tired, Rachel encourages Jamie to help her hold his bottle. Towards the end of his bottle Jamie is falling asleep so Rachel wipes his face clean with his bib and wraps him in a sheet before lying him down on the floor cushion. She sits with him for a few short minutes until he falls asleep.	HEA4 HEA8 HEA14
1:15	Jamie wakes up before most of the other children and is waving his arms to attract somebody. Sarah picks him up and sits him on her knee. Talking to him, he is struggling to see her face from his angle, so she turns him around and balances him on the end of her knees. She bounces him up and down gently and mimics his facial expressions for quite some time. As other children wake gradually, Sarah sits them in their favourite chairs and cushions in a circle and moves down to join them on the floor, offering each of the young babies a choice from a selection of fabric and board books in her hands for them to enjoy.	HEA10

Time	Activity	Achieved
2:00	The activity planned for this afternoon is shredded paper play. The older children have a huge pile of shredded paper to run or crawl through, but Rachel has saved a small pile to put in Jamie's inflatable ring and he clearly enjoys the whole session. He waves his hands in it, kicks his feet and rubs it into his face, chewing on some of it. Rachel watches him closely and takes the pieces from his mouth before any gets eaten.	**HEA3**
3:00	Afternoon snack is cream cheese sandwiches in narrow cut fingers so Jamie gets stuck in, squidging his fingers in it and rubbing it into his face as he tastes it. He is clearly enjoying himself when his mum arrives to pick him up. She sits alongside Rachel on the floor waiting for Jamie to finish his snack, giving Mum and Rachel a great opportunity to catch up before he leaves for the day.	**HEA8**

Code list	Additional suggestions
A Strong Child	
HEA1 Me, Myself and I	Musical toys; Water play.
HEA2 Being Acknowledged and Affirmed	Peek-a-boo; Hand puppets.
HEA3 Developing Self-assurance	Sand play; Sitting in the ball pool.
HEA4 A Sense of Belonging	Singing lullabies; Watching fish in tank.
A Skilful Communicator	
HEA5 Being Together	Relaxing changing time; Sharing cuddly toys.
HEA6 Finding a Voice	Let's all shout loud; Mimicking hummed tunes.
HEA7 Listening and Responding	Can you hear me over here?; Making funny noises.
HEA8 Making Meaning	Sleep time with a favourite comforter; Leaving Mum/Dad in the morning.
A Competent Learner	
HEA9 Making Connections	Walking to the shops; Exploring a favourite person.
HEA10 Being Imaginative	A family grouped session; A musical session.
HEA11 Being Creative	A feely session with textured fabrics; Joining in with different types of music.
HEA12 Representing	Finger painting; Sand in a shallow tray.
A Healthy Child	
HEA13 Emotional Well-being	Sharing a story; Snack with Mum and key worker.
HEA14 Growing and Developing	Finger food; Different teething rings;
HEA15 Keeping Safe	Practising sitting; Stretching my legs.
HEA16 Healthy Choices	Heuristic play; Choosing milk or juice.

Aspect title: Component title:		Code =
Development matters		**Play and practical support**

Sample activity	
Resources	
Health and safety	
Layout	
The role of the key worker	
Note	
Questions to ask/ suggested interactions	• .
Comments	

Ⓟ

Heads Up, Lookers and Communicators

Completed by: **Date:**

Heads Up, Lookers and Communicators
(0–8 months)

Date of activity:	Supervised by:

Children involved:

Comments

Date of activity:	Supervised by:

Children involved:

Comments

Date of activity:	Supervised by:

Children involved:

Comments

(P)

Sitters, Standers
and
Explorers

(8–18 months)

Sitters, Standers and Explorers
(8–18 months)

Section index

Notes for this section

It is tempting to start this section by telling you how demanding children are in this age group. Strictly speaking, you do not need to be told this for two important reasons. Firstly, all of our children have a right to expect as much of our time and concentration as we can give them and, secondly, you will already know about the rapidly increasing demands of this group. Eight to 18 months is a huge gap in terms of physical and emotional development – so what might suit your less mobile eight-month-old is likely to need adjustment to suit your speedy 18-month-old.

Ofsted suggest a minimum child:staff ratio of three babies to each adult and this is for a good reason. Each of the babies in your group will demand a lot of your time, so think carefully about the implications of this when planning your activity. There will be certain activities much better carried out on a 1:1 basis. Work with colleagues to help achieve this for your sessions and, of course, offer them the same facility when it is time for their planning too.

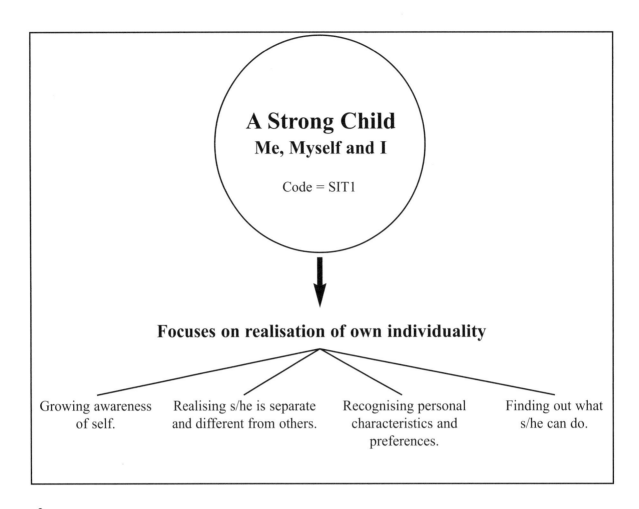

A Strong Child
Me, Myself and I

Code = SIT1

Focuses on realisation of own individuality

Growing awareness of self.

Realising s/he is separate and different from others.

Recognising personal characteristics and preferences.

Finding out what s/he can do.

Development matters

Babies develop an understanding and awareness of themselves which is influenced by their family, culture, other people and the environment.

Look, listen, note

Note how babies use the opportunities you provide to develop, show and communicate their preferences and decisions.

Effective practice

Playfully helping babies to recognise that they are separate and different from others, e.g. adult pointing to own and baby's nose, eyes, finger, toes.

Play and practical support

Provide a variety of mirrors in different places to help babies explore what they look like and who they are.

Sitters, Standers and Explorers

A Strong Child
Me, Myself and I

Code = SIT1

Development matters	Play and practical support
Babies develop an understanding and awareness of themselves which is influenced by their family, culture, other people and the environment.	Provide a variety of mirrors in different places to help babies explore what they look like and who they are.

Sample activity	Recognising me!
Resources	Child-safe mirrors, reflective surfaces, and a key worker with time for fun and quiet reflection.
Health and safety	Ensure that mirrors selected are appropriate for the age group and that freestanding mirrors are properly supported.
Layout	Prepare the room/area with mirrors and reflective surfaces of many different types – freestanding mirrors that we can see behind, mirrors to hold, large mirrors to see both of our faces at the same time, mirrors we can walk towards, lie underneath and mirrors that we can cover with sheet for peek-a-boo play.
The role of the key worker	Sit quietly at the child's level and observe. Watch how they use things near to them and where their gaze strays to. Talk with them about what they see and about what they are doing. Encourage them to look at the mirrors in different ways, perhaps using the mirrors to direct the gaze of babies. Share the mirrors with them, encouraging them to look at their own face as well as your own or those of other children. Change the mirrors for different types intermittently, allowing exploration without allowing the child to become bored with the same activity. Use the mirrors to reinforce positive self-image even in very young babies, describing beautiful brown eyes or lovely curly hair, for example.
Note	Note how babies use the opportunities you provide, to develop, show and communicate their preferences and decisions.
Questions to ask/ suggested interactions	• Who can you see in the mirror? • Where's James? • Where's James's nose?
Comments	This was a very relaxing and enjoyable session that would definitely benefit from repeat sessions. More could have been achieved with a larger variety of mirrors, so will borrow more mirrors from other rooms for the next session.

Sitters, Standers and Explorers

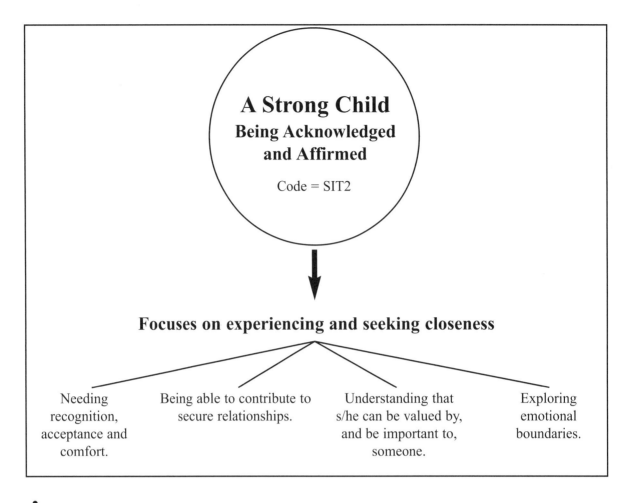

A Strong Child
Being Acknowledged and Affirmed

Code = SIT2

Focuses on experiencing and seeking closeness

Needing recognition, acceptance and comfort.

Being able to contribute to secure relationships.

Understanding that s/he can be valued by, and be important to, someone.

Exploring emotional boundaries.

Development matters	Babies seek to gain attention in a variety of ways.
Look, listen, note	Note whether babies are able to be physically close and enjoy being with you.
Effective practice	Actively listen and give your full attention when babies communicate with you.
Play and practical support	When communicating with babies, crouch down to their level to establish and maintain contact with eye, voice or light touch.

Sitters, Standers and Explorers

A Strong Child

Being Acknowledged and Affirmed

Code = SIT2

Development matters	Play and practical support
Babies seek to gain attention in a variety of ways.	When communicating with babies, crouch down to their level to establish and maintain contact with eye, voice or light touch.

Sample activity	Peek-a-boo.
Resources	Nothing specific is necessary – just use what you have on hand.
Health and safety	There are no health and safety risks to this activity.
Layout	No particular layout is necessary, but it will work better if you are at a distance from the child.
The role of the key worker	Sit watching the children in your group and seek to make eye contact with one of them. As they catch your eye, hide behind your hand, but peek around to see if they are still watching. Smile so that they know you are playing, but hide again, perhaps this time behind a toy or book. If the baby does not begin to move nearer to you, shuffle slightly nearer to them yourself. Keep changing the shield that you hide behind and moving nearer until the baby begins to move towards you. Keep playing until the baby is near enough to snatch up in a cuddle and a tickle.
Note	Note whether babies are able to be physically close and enjoy being with you.
Questions to ask/ suggested interactions	• Where's Helen gone? Here I am! • Try to make much of the game non-verbal.
Comments	Take care not to lose the baby's interest at the beginning by firmly reintroducing eye contact each time you come from behind your shield, smiling at the baby or babies playing. Try to play this right the way across the room to encourage a feeling of security that does not rely on proximity.

Sitters, Standers and Explorers

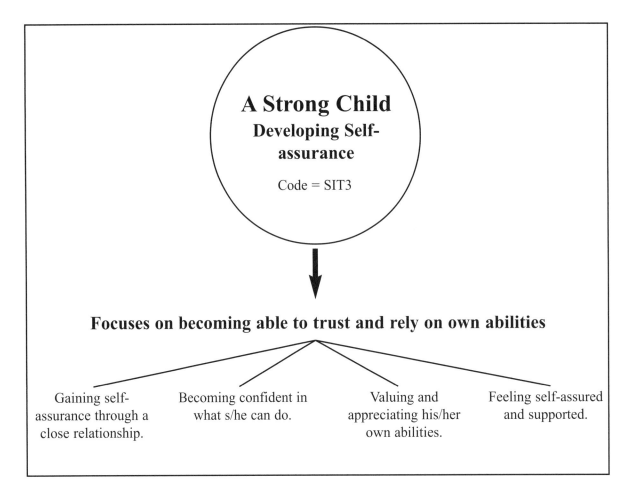

A Strong Child
Developing Self-assurance

Code = SIT3

Focuses on becoming able to trust and rely on own abilities

| Gaining self-assurance through a close relationship. | Becoming confident in what s/he can do. | Valuing and appreciating his/her own abilities. | Feeling self-assured and supported. |

Development matters

To develop independence babies need to feel safe and secure within healthy relationships with key people.

Look, listen, note

Note how babies become confident in exploring what they can do with less dependence on adults.

Effective practice

Provide accessible resources so that babies can choose what they need to begin an activity independently.

Play and practical support

Increase the time babies play independently, remembering it is comforting for them to hear familiar sounds and have you near.

Sitters, Standers and Explorers

A Strong Child
Developing Self-assurance

Development matters	Play and practical support
To develop independence babies need to feel safe and secure within healthy relationships with key people.	Increase the time babies play independently, remembering it is comforting for them to hear familiar sounds and have you near.

Sample activity	What can we find?
Resources	A box of safe bits and pieces – assorted different bits of toys or teddies etc.
Health and safety	Ensure that items in the box are appropriate to the child's age. Watch carefully to ensure that the box does not topple or the baby does not fall into the box.
Layout	Set the box out on a clear space on the floor and sit alongside it.
The role of the key worker	Sit quietly, looking carefully and rummaging in the box. As you get the attention of one or two babies ask them if they would like to join you, inviting all who pay attention. Encourage them to look for what they can find in the box, but as they begin to enjoy themselves sit to one side and leave them to it. As individual babies look to you for attention respond positively and verbally, but stay at a distance to encourage independent exploration to continue. Ensure that toys discarded by one child are carefully replaced back in the box for others to enjoy, but without interfering. Watch closely to prevent quarrels, distracting individuals away from a fought after toy.
Note	Note how babies become confident in exploring what they can do with less dependence on adults.
Questions to ask/ suggested interactions	• What can we see in this box? • Can Andrew find the blue teddy? • Shall we let Alexandra play with that shell while we look for the car?
Comments	It might be sensible to start this activity in a separate room with a few select children, selected in order to avoid fighting over popular items. Take care not to participate more than is necessary, withdrawing participation further with repeated activities. Remember that the same box of toys will not encourage individual exploration each time. Deliberately use different toys, different boxes and different times of the day to encourage further exploration.

Sitters, Standers and Explorers

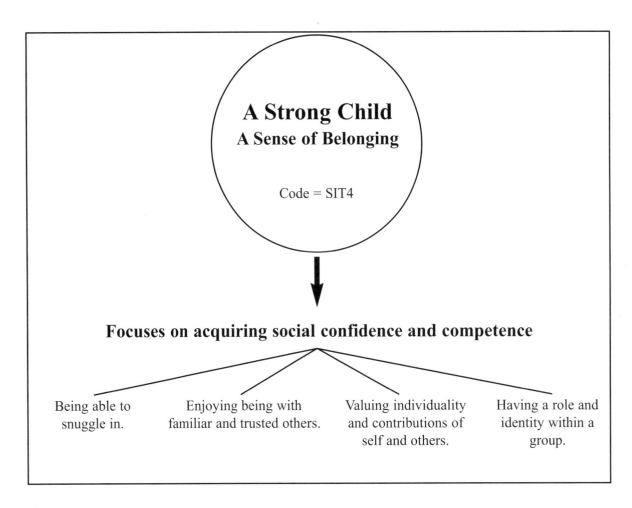

A Strong Child
A Sense of Belonging

Code = SIT4

↓

Focuses on acquiring social confidence and competence

| Being able to snuggle in. | Enjoying being with familiar and trusted others. | Valuing individuality and contributions of self and others. | Having a role and identity within a group. |

Development matters

To sustain healthy emotional attachments babies need familiar, trusting, safe and secure relationships.

Look, listen, note

Note the ways you nurture babies' sense of themselves while also helping them feel they belong to the group.

Effective practice

At times of transition (such as the beginning or end of the day or change of shifts) greet and say goodbye to babies and their parents. This helps to develop secure and trusting three-way relationships.

Play and practical support

Provide experiences that involve using all the senses, such as relaxing music, soft lighting and pleasant smells for babies to enjoy.

Sitters, Standers and Explorers

A Strong Child

A Sense of Belonging

Development matters	Play and practical support
To sustain healthy emotional attachments babies need familiar, trusting, safe and secure relationships.	Provide experiences that involve using all of the senses, such as relaxing music, soft lighting and pleasant smells for the babies to enjoy.

Sample activity	Washing ourselves.
Resources	A low and secure water container that the babies can sit in safely. Bubble bath from a recognised children's range. Plenty of towels and face cloths. A relaxing CD to set the mood.
Health and safety	Ensure that supervision is appropriate to ensure that the water presents no risk of drowning and that the additional products used present no allergic threat to the baby.
Layout	Fill the container (to a safe level) with warm water, spreading some towels around the tub to soak up spills.
The role of the key worker	Select two or three babies who get along with each other and dress them carefully in a suitable swimming nappy or similar. Get the support of another worker from the group. Sit the babies in the tub before adding the bubble bath and encourage them to feel relaxed. Gently scoop the water over the arms of the babies to ascertain that they feel comfortable with this type of play. Introduce the bubble bath by squirting some on your own hands, rubbing them together to show the babies the bubbles created. Smooth your hands over the legs of the babies, talking about the softness and the bubbles. Shake your hands in the water, making more bubbles. Talk to the babies throughout, encouraging them to splash gently and enjoy the experience.
Note	Note the ways you nurture babies' sense of themselves while also helping them feel they belong to the group.
Questions to ask/ suggested interactions	• Can you shake your hands and make more bubbles? • Is that fun? • Does that water feel nice running down your arms?
Comments	Remember to keep the session short enough to ensure that the water does not get too cold.

Sitters, Standers and Explorers

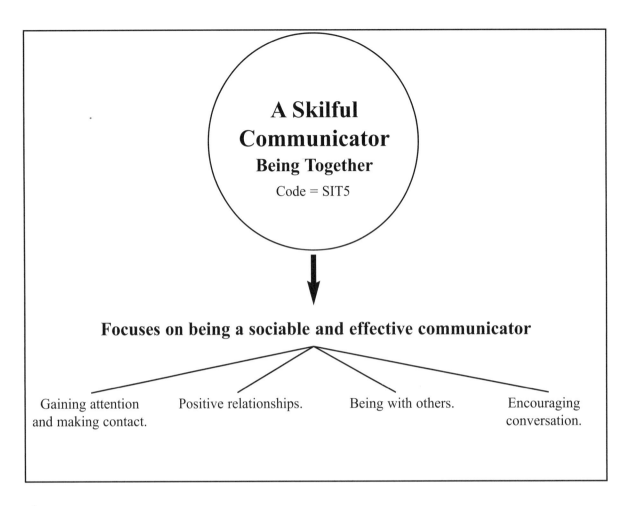

A Skilful
Communicator
Being Together
Code = SIT5

Focuses on being a sociable and effective communicator

Gaining attention
and making contact.

Positive relationships.

Being with others.

Encouraging
conversation.

Development matters	Babies use their developing physical skills to make social contact.
Look, listen, note	Listen to the sounds babies make and the words children use as they make friends, noting differences in the way they communicate with adults and other children.
Effective practice	Ensure there is good communication between parents and practitioners to provide babies and children with positive models.
Play and practical support	'What is it?' is one of the earliest questions as a baby holds up an object, accompanied by a questioning facial expression. Provide interesting objects such as a squeaky toy.

Sitters, Standers and Explorers

A Skilful Communicator
Being Together

Development matters	Play and practical support
Babies use their developing physical skills to make social contact.	'What is it?' is one of the earliest questions as a baby holds up an object, accompanied by a questioning facial expression. Provide interesting objects such as a squeaky toy.

Sample activity	Can you find …?
Resources	Make use of the items generally scattered around a room.
Health and safety	Ensure that requests made of the babies are reasonable and possible for the babies to achieve, with no risk of furniture toppling as babies pull themselves up on things.
Layout	Make sure that there are a selection of items that the children in your group can reach by their chosen method of travel – shuffling, crawling, walking etc.
The role of the key worker	Sitting on the floor, ask one of your group: 'Can you pass me that Elmo?', praising them when they do. As others become interested, ask for different things from around the room, pointing in the right direction if they look confused. Try also to remember things from different heights to give each of the babies involved a challenge for their next step.
Note	Listen to the sounds babies make and the words children use as they make friends, noting differences in the way they communicate with adults and other children.
Questions to ask/ suggested interactions	• Who can find the blue car? • Can Gabriel pass Andrew the big teddy? • Can Hope reach the tambourine?
Comments	Try to give each of the children involved something readily achievable, to foster the feeling of satisfaction. After this try to give each of the children a task that prompts them to try something a little more than they would normally achieve. Offer them support if they are trying to stand up against the table, or reach something challenging.

Sitters, Standers and Explorers

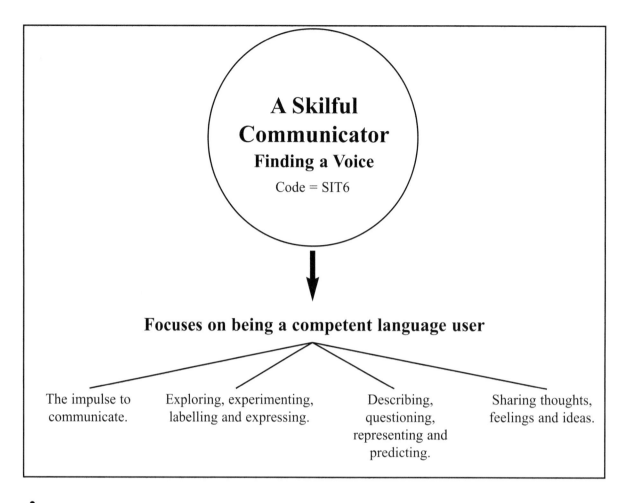

A Skilful Communicator
Finding a Voice
Code = SIT6

Focuses on being a competent language user

The impulse to communicate.

Exploring, experimenting, labelling and expressing.

Describing, questioning, representing and predicting.

Sharing thoughts, feelings and ideas.

Development matters	Babies enjoy experimenting, exploring and using sounds and words to represent objects around them.
Look, listen, note	Listen to the sounds and early words babies use and how familiar adults show that they understand them.
Effective practice	Sharing the fun of discovery and valuing babies' words, e.g. by bringing the doll in response to 'baba'.
Play and practical support	Encourage exploration and imitation of sound by providing objects such as firmly sealed yoghurt pots or plastic bottles filled with water, sand, gravel.

Sitters, Standers and Explorers

A Skilful Communicator

Finding a Voice

Development matters	Play and practical support
Babies enjoy experimenting, exploring and using sounds and words to represent objects around them.	Encourage exploration and imitation of sound by providing objects such as firmly sealed yoghurt pots or plastic bottles filled with water, sand, gravel.

Sample activity	Making music from everyday objects.
Resources	Gather together a selection of things that make interesting sounds but are, of course, safe for this age group.
Health and safety	There are no health and safety risks to this activity.
Layout	Clear an area on the floor or on a table and lay out a selection of items in the centre, with space for the babies to sit around the outside in a comfortable circle or pop in and out as interest comes and goes.
The role of the key worker	After selection of items, catch the attention of one of your group and ask them if they can make a particular sound. Watch as they try to imitate the sound that you have made with that object, offering support to shake their hand in the same way as your own, for example. As others join or interest is maintained, switch items and try to make different kinds of sounds. Use a balloon, a pan, an empty box as a drum, comparing the sound of each as you go along. Encourage the group to strike the instruments with their hands or a wooden spoon, even a dummy to explore different sounds.
Note	Listen to the sounds and early words babies use and how familiar adults show that they understand them.
Questions to ask/ suggested interactions	• Can Isabel shake this bottle like Jayne? • Can we bang this pan gently? • Now let's bang it as loud as we can.
Comments	Try to use different groups of instruments at different sessions, even sometimes using items that don't make sound but suggest them, such as farm animals, demonstrating that cows moo etc.

Sitters, Standers and Explorers

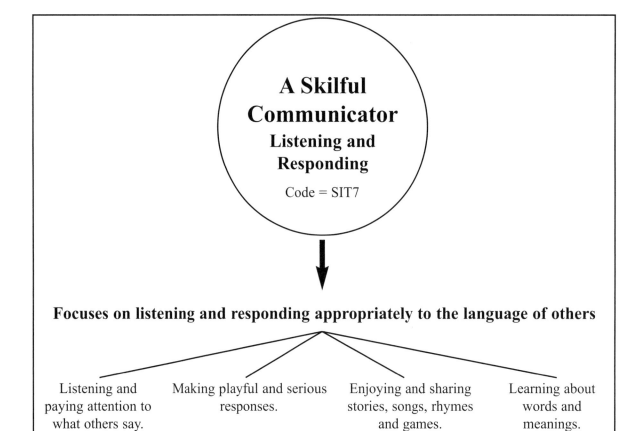

A Skilful
Communicator
Listening and
Responding

Code = SIT7

Focuses on listening and responding appropriately to the language of others

Listening and paying attention to what others say.

Making playful and serious responses.

Enjoying and sharing stories, songs, rhymes and games.

Learning about words and meanings.

Development matters

In a familiar context, with a key person, babies can understand and respond to the different things said to them.

Look, listen, note

Note the ways in which babies show you they have understood your request and note their responses to you.

Effective practice

Talk to babies about what you are doing throughout the day, so they will link words with actions, e.g. welcoming, preparing lunch.

Play and practical support

Provide tapes of rhymes and stories, sounds and spoken words – some that require young babies to respond, others that engage them to listen.

Sitters, Standers and Explorers

A Skilful Communicator
Listening and Responding

Development matters	Play and practical support
In a familiar context, with a key person, babies can understand and respond to different things said to them.	Provide tapes of rhymes and stories, sounds and spoken words – some that require young babies to respond, others that encourage them to listen.

Sample activity	Listening to music and joining in.
Resources	A tape/CD with songs such as 'Old Macdonald had a farm' or 'Heads and shoulders, knees and toes'.
Health and safety	There are no health and safety risks to this activity.
Layout	Place the tape/CD player near to the key worker so that popular songs can be repeated again and again to the children's satisfaction.
The role of the key worker	Sit with a small group of babies and select a song to start the session that you know your group are familiar with, but do not sing along yourself. Getting the group's attention, encourage them to listen to the music, asking: 'Whats that she's singing?', perhaps pointing to the speakers. If the children join in, use huge amounts of praise to encourage them to continue. If they do not appear to have made the connection, ask related questions such as: 'What does the cow say?' and wait for the moo sound to come from the tape/CD. Repeat the same song several times until the children are beginning to join in before moving on to the next song.
Note	Note the ways in which babies show you they have understood your request and note their responses to you.
Questions to ask/ suggested interactions	• Can you hear what the lady is singing? • What sound does the cow make? • Can we join in this time?
Comments	Try not to move too quickly with this activity, allowing the recognition of the children to dictate when to move on. Do not be surprised if younger babies in this group cannot make the connection without participation of the older children in this group. Mixed ability groups will benefit from the continuation of this activity, encouraging younger children to take to it a little sooner than they may otherwise do.

Sitters, Standers and Explorers

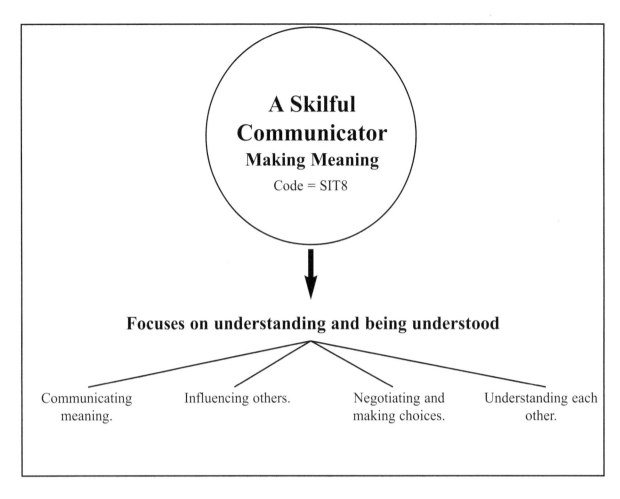

A Skilful
Communicator
Making Meaning
Code = SIT8

Focuses on understanding and being understood

Communicating meaning.

Influencing others.

Negotiating and making choices.

Understanding each other.

Development matters

Babies learn that their voice and actions have an effect on others and they strive to share meanings.

Look, listen, note

Try to understand and note the personal words babies create as they begin to develop language.

Effective practice

Respond to what babies show you they're interested in and want to do by providing activities, stories and games.

Play and practical support

Provide opportunities for babies to make choices, e.g. which spoon to choose, which bib to wear, the size of paintbrush to use, to go outdoors or stay in.

Sitters, Standers and Explorers

A Skilful Communicator
Making Meaning

Code = SIT8

Development matters	Play and practical support
Babies learn that their voice and actions have an effect on others and they strive to share meanings.	Provide opportunities for babies to make choices, e.g. which spoon to choose, which bib to wear, the size of the paintbrush to use, to go outdoors or to stay in.

Sample activity	Making choices at snack time.
Resources	A snack that provides choice, such as white or brown, triangular or square sandwiches. A selection of bibs and cups/beakers to drink from.
Health and safety	Ensure that food, bibs, beakers etc. are commensurate with babies' ages and requirements.
Layout	Sit the babies around the table or in their high chairs in a semicircle in company with those around the table.
The role of the key worker	Sitting talking with your group, place a selection of bibs in front of the children and encourage the children to select their own bib. Help the older children put on their bibs. Once ready to eat, hold a different sandwich in each hand and ask each child in turn which sandwich they would prefer, being quite specific about the choices available: 'Would you like a brown cheese sandwich or a white tuna one?', emphasising each sandwich as they are offered. Encourage older children to identify their preferences vocally, saying just 'white' or 'brown', while younger children can show their preferences by pointing or gesturing. Try to make options available whenever possible so that the children will understand (eventually) that sometimes there is choice, but sometimes there isn't.
Note	Try to understand and note the personal words babies create as they begin to develop language.
Questions to ask/ suggested interactions	• Would you like a square sandwich or a triangular one? • Do you want tuna or egg? • Shall I help you with that bib?
Comments	Offer babies choices that are commensurate with their age and stage of development, but do remember to talk about the choices available even with younger babies in this group.

Sitters, Standers and Explorers

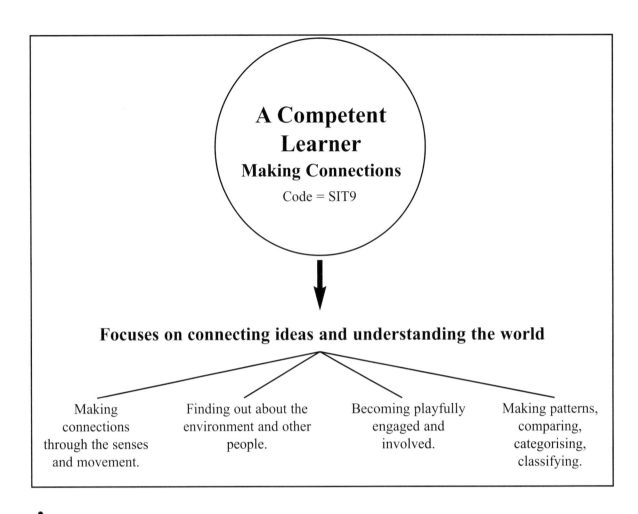

**A Competent
Learner**
Making Connections
Code = SIT9

Focuses on connecting ideas and understanding the world

| Making connections through the senses and movement. | Finding out about the environment and other people. | Becoming playfully engaged and involved. | Making patterns, comparing, categorising, classifying. |

Development matters As they become more mobile, babies connect with toys, objects and a wider group of people.

Look, listen, note How a baby explores open-ended resources such as cardboard boxes, tubing, floaty scarves.

Effective practice Accept each baby's pace of learning and give them time to make connections.

Play and practical support Provide resources for babies to play with, e.g. pots and pans, wooden blocks, soft toys.

Sitters, Standers and Explorers

A Competent Learner
Making Connections

Development matters	Play and practical support
As they become more mobile, babies connect with toys, objects and a wider group of people.	Provide resources for babies to play with, e.g. pots and pans, wooden blocks, soft toys etc.

Sample activity	Role playing making tea.
Resources	A selection of pots, pans, cups, saucers, spoons and cooking equipment from the home corner. A representation of a cooker and sink is useful but not vital.
Health and safety	Make sure that water spilt does not present a risk of slipping.
Layout	Set out the table in your preferred format, perhaps using the tea set, with teapot for one session, the cooking materials for a different session.
The role of the key worker	Sitting with your tea set, pour one of your group a cup of tea and ask them if they'd like one. Encourage the children in your group to pour a cup for you, or another in the group, matching cups to saucers etc. Remember to stir in the milk, sugar etc. talking throughout about what you are doing.
Note	Note how a baby follows any particular order – tea, sugar, milk etc. before stirring the cup.
Questions to ask/ suggested interactions	• Who would like a cup of tea? • Would you like milk in your tea? • Can we match this blue cup with a blue saucer?
Comments	Vary the activity when circumstances permit by using water in the teapot, possibly milk in the milk jug etc.

Sitters, Standers and Explorers

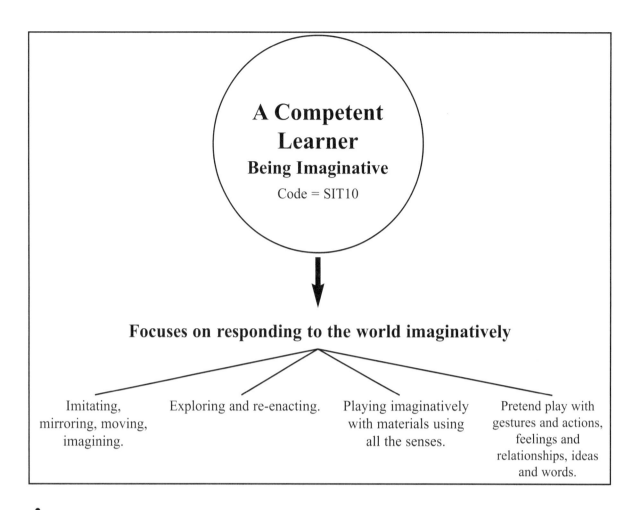

A Competent Learner
Being Imaginative
Code = SIT10

Focuses on responding to the world imaginatively

Imitating, mirroring, moving, imagining.

Exploring and re-enacting.

Playing imaginatively with materials using all the senses.

Pretend play with gestures and actions, feelings and relationships, ideas and words.

Development matters	As they become mobile, babies use their whole bodies to recreate an experience.
Look, listen, note	Note the differences between babies' imitations and the bodily movements which they use to recreate a situation, e.g. bouncing on the adults knee.
Effective practice	Imaginative opportunities for babies to explore movement and materials which use all the senses, both alone and in a group.
Play and practical support	Discover from parents the imitative games their babies enjoy and use them as the basis of your play.

Sitters, Standers and Explorers

A Competent Learner
Being Imaginative

Code = SIT10

Development matters	Play and practical support
As they become mobile, babies use their whole bodies to recreate an experience.	Discover from parents the imitative games their babies enjoy and use them as the basis of your play.

Sample activity	A very messy painting session.
Resources	A large empty tub such as a flat sand or water tray. Thick paint or coloured gloop. Large pieces of paper such as the reverse side of wallpaper. A table/work surface at the same height as the empty tub.
Health and safety	Make sure that products used do not present allergy risks to the babies involved. Babies will need to be supported to ensure that slippery paint/gloop etc. does not make them fall over.
Layout	Lay the table at the side of the tub to make an L shape. Put your paint/gloop into the tub and tape the paper onto the table. Lots of protective clothing for everybody participating, or babies stripped to just nappies.
The role of the key worker	The most important thing in this session is to be as flexible as possible! Encourage the baby participating to explore the paint in any way she feels comfortable, but show her that painting on the lovely big piece of paper is a part of the activity, not something she might get into trouble doing. Encourage her to make patterns with her hands, whole arms, and even her torso or whole body if she chooses to climb in! Whichever method she prefers to explore the paint, try to offer the same method of making her mark on the paper. This may mean asking a colleague to remove the table, but tape the paper directly onto the floor so that she can sit or lie on it. Try not to direct her play too much, limiting your input to suggesting different methods to try.
Note	Note the differences between babies' imitations and the bodily movements which they use to recreate a situation, e.g. bouncing on the adult's knee.
Questions to ask/ suggested interactions	• How does that feel on your fingers? • Why not try your whole arms? • Can we make patterns with those arms on this paper?
Comments	This is not an activity for the faint-hearted! Try this when your numbers are low, or when you have the extra support of volunteers or helpers to avoid ending up with paint all over everybody else's clothing.

Sitters, Standers and Explorers

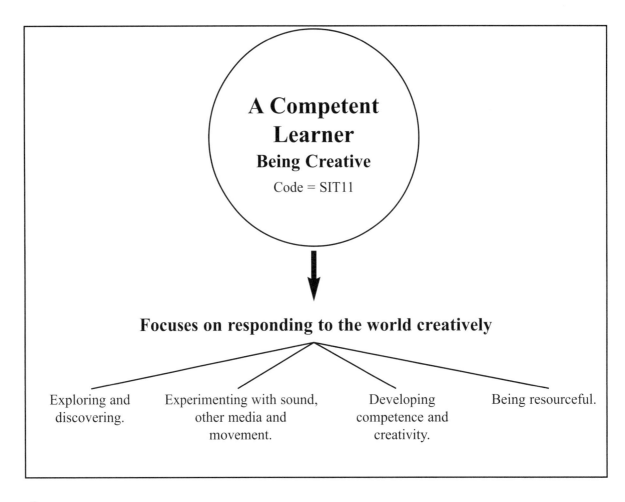

A Competent
Learner
Being Creative
Code = SIT11

Focuses on responding to the world creatively

Exploring and
discovering.

Experimenting with sound,
other media and
movement.

Developing
competence and
creativity.

Being resourceful.

Development matters

Babies quickly make sense of and respond to what they see, hear, feel, touch and smell.

Look, listen, note

Observe the movements and sounds babies make as they explore materials such as musical instruments, paint, dough, glue and the space around them.

Effective practice

Provide opportunities for creative physical experiences for babies, such as bouncing, rolling and splashing both indoors and outdoors.

Play and practical support

Materials such as finger paint, PVA glue and wet play give babies the opportunity to delight in sensory exploration and mess-making.

Sitters, Standers and Explorers

A Competent Learner
Being Creative

Code = SIT11

Development matters	Play and practical support
Babies quickly make sense of and respond to what they see, hear, feel, touch and smell.	Materials such as finger paint, PVA glue and wet play give babies the opportunity to delight in sensory exploration and mess-making.

Sample activity	Making a tactile collage.
Resources	Heavyweight card from inside cereal boxes etc to stick your collage materials to. A variety of tubs containing different types of collage materials such as shredded paper, cornflakes, pasta shapes including long sticks of spaghetti, different coloured tiny circles from hole punching, scented sticks of rosemary or sage from the garden etc. PVA glue in a flat open tray. Big aprons.
Health and safety	Ensure that products used do not present a risk of allergic reaction. PVA should be safe for use, but may present problems if fingers are sucked etc.
Layout	Sit your child securely at the table in front of their piece of card which has been taped to the table, with the tub of PVA to their preferred side and tubs of collage materials around the edge.
The role of the key worker	Encourage the child to spread the PVA over the card using their whole hand, observing how they react when the glue starts sticking to things. Depending on this reaction you may wish to remove the PVA and wipe their hands before offering them the tubs of collage materials, or you may prefer to leave them to it. Explain/show her that you want her to stick things onto the card, but then take a step back and leave her to attempt it herself. Take care to intervene if she is distressed by things sticking to her hands rather than the paper, wiping her hand if this is distracting her from the activity.
Note	Observe the movements and sounds babies make as they explore materials such as paint, dough, glue and the space around them.
Questions to ask/ suggested interactions	• Can you put lots of this sticky glue onto the paper? • What shall we stick on first? • Would you like me to wipe those sticky fingers?
Comments	Not all children will feel comfortable with this level of mess, so take care to introduce this gradually for those you feel may not like it.

Sitters, Standers and Explorers

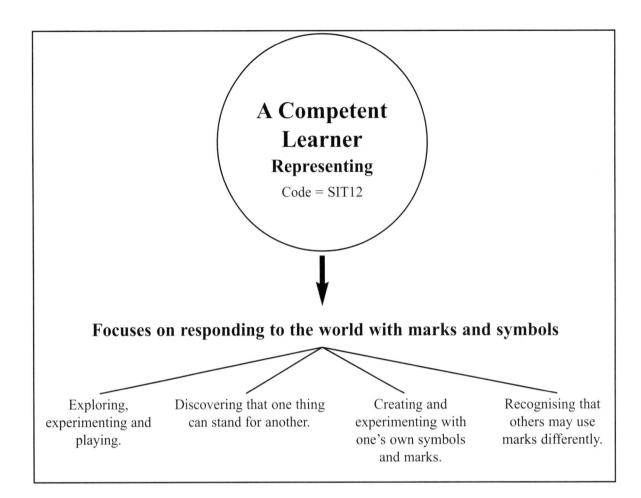

A Competent Learner
Representing
Code = SIT12

Focuses on responding to the world with marks and symbols

Exploring, experimenting and playing.

Discovering that one thing can stand for another.

Creating and experimenting with one's own symbols and marks.

Recognising that others may use marks differently.

Development matters

Babies imitate and improvise actions they have observed – a scarf is made to stand for a blanket or a plastic cone for a microphone.

Look, listen, note

Observe the early marks babies and children make when given a crayon or brush for the first time.

Effective practice

Provide varied resources to anticipate what babies and children might need to represent their experiences.

Play and practical support

Draw attention to marks, signs and symbols in the environment and talk about what they represent.

Sitters, Standers and Explorers

A Competent Learner
Representing

Development matters	Play and practical support
Babies imitate and improvise actions they have observed – a scarf is made to stand for a blanket or a plastic cone for a microphone.	Provide varied resources to anticipate what babies and children might need to represent their experiences.

Sample activity	Dressing up.
Resources	A selection of items that the babies can use without adult intervention, such as scarves, hats, bags, ties, shawls. Set alongside it a selection of domestic items such as a telephone, dolls' prams and cots. A selection of dolls or teddies.
Health and safety	Ensure that scarves etc. are carefully watched to ensure no risk of strangulation.
Layout	Arrange the objects so that some are laid out over the chair or cushions, but some remain in the box to encourage exploration.
The role of the key worker	Watch to see the babies select items that they can use to represent things from home. Try not to intervene, but if play starts a little slowly you could receive a phone call from Mum and pass it on, or use a scarf to wrap the baby in. Watch how the babies use the items provided, trying to vary items on each occasion.
Note	Note examples of young children using one thing to stand for another, e.g. a box for a car.
Questions to ask/ suggested interactions	• Is that Laura's mum? Would you like to speak to her? • Why don't we take the babies for a walk in our prams? • Who wears something like this that we know?
Comments	Try to avoid clothing that babies need help to put on, although for older children in this age group the additional challenge will be welcome.

Sitters, Standers and Explorers

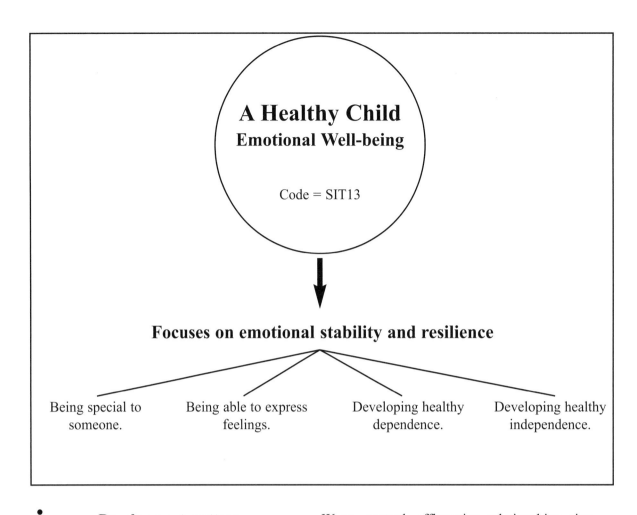

A Healthy Child
Emotional Well-being

Code = SIT13

Focuses on emotional stability and resilience

Being special to someone.

Being able to express feelings.

Developing healthy dependence.

Developing healthy independence.

Development matters	Warm, mutual, affirmative relationships give babies the courage to express their feelings.
Look, listen, note	Note verbal and non-verbal expressions of feelings which take place when babies are changed, fed, cuddled etc.
Effective practice	Establish shared understandings between home and setting about ways of responding to babies' emotions.
Play and practical support	Collect and share stories and songs which parents and babies use at home.

Sitters, Standers and Explorers

A Healthy Child
Emotional Well-being

Code = SIT13

Development matters	Play and practical support
Warm, mutual, affirmative relationships give babies the courage to express their feelings.	Collect and share stories and songs which parents and babies use at home.

Sample activity	Welcome to nursery.
Resources	Your knowledge of the families in your group and the day book/diary etc.
Health and safety	There are no health and safety risks to this activity.
Layout	Nothing specific required, just a warm and welcoming environment.
The role of the key worker	Make sure that you recognise and welcome each of the children into your room each session, paying special attention to the children from your key group. Make your welcome warm, using the parent's preferred name and the child's name, and ask: 'How are you both today?' or 'Did you have a good weekend?' etc. Take care to note down comments that may impact on the child's day, such as a disturbed night, a new tooth coming through etc. Where applicable, take the child from the parent with a big hug, or welcome them with a hug if they have arrived on foot.
Note	Note verbal and non-verbal expressions of feeling which take place when babies are changed, fed, cuddled etc.
Questions to ask/ suggested interactions	• Did you sing your lovely song to Mummy last night? • Are you a tired boy already? • Ask Mum/Dad what they did to calm the child etc.
Comments	It is vital that as a key worker you build up strong relationships with families from your key group, but not to the exclusion of others in the same environment. Remember that if a colleague is absent you will be sharing the care of their group temporarily, so it will be important that a relationship is established with all families to some extent. Talking with parents of young babies is the most important way of gathering facts about things that go on at home that may help with your care of the child. A new baby or visiting relative might impact on a normal sleep pattern etc.

Sitters, Standers and Explorers

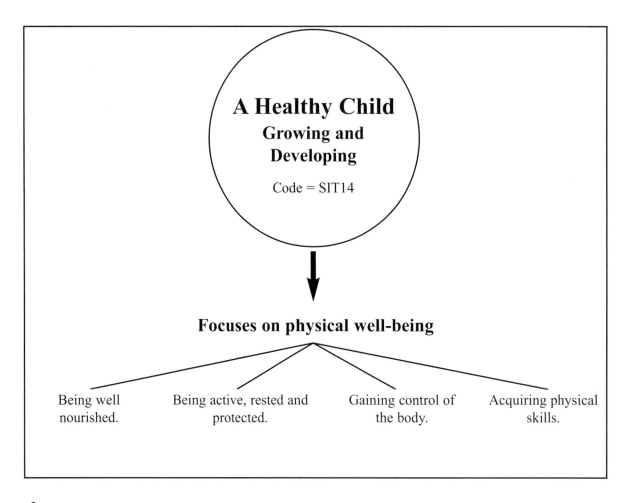

A Healthy Child
Growing and Developing

Code = SIT14

Focuses on physical well-being

Being well nourished.

Being active, rested and protected.

Gaining control of the body.

Acquiring physical skills.

Development matters	For babies and children, rest and sleep are as important as food.
Look, listen, note	Observe how babies' behaviour changes as they get tired and require sleep.
Effective practice	Treat meal times as an opportunity to help children to enjoy their food and become independent in feeding themselves. Learn to recognise the signs of tiredness in babies, children and adults.
Play and practical support	Provide a comfortable and accessible place where babies can rest or sleep when they want to.

Sitters, Standers and Explorers

A Healthy Child
Growing and Developing

Code = SIT14

Development matters	Play and practical support
For babies and children, rest and sleep are as important as food.	Provide a comfortable and accessible place where babies can rest or sleep when they want to.

Sample activity	Getting ready for a nap.
Resources	A comfy place to sleep such as a dark and quiet room.
Health and safety	Ensure that all normal sleep checks are carried out.
Layout	Lay the room out with plenty of space for each of the tired babies, with floor cushions covered with a clean sheet and a warm blanket to wrap the baby in. Use calming music. Make sure you have the baby's preferred comforter(s).
The role of the key worker	Adopt a calm and relaxing manner while preparing the room for nap time. Select a calming CD with the volume low. Prepare the baby for sleep in a calm, unhurried manner, trying to talk quietly and calmly without engaging the baby in chat. Gather together his comforters, blanket, dummy, teddy etc. and wrap him securely in a sheet. Lay him down, covering him with his blanket. Sit next to him, or nearby, perhaps stroking his cheek if that comforts him.
Note	Observe how babies' behaviour changes as they get tired and require sleep.
Questions to ask/ suggested interactions	• Try not to ask any questions at all during this period.
Comments	Observation of your key group should inform you of their preferred sleep time habits. Note them down carefully in case others may be caring for them at different times. If the child's usual pattern becomes disrupted, chat with parents or other carers to identify if a change has been identified at home or elsewhere and consider adapting your daytime routine accordingly.

Sitters, Standers and Explorers

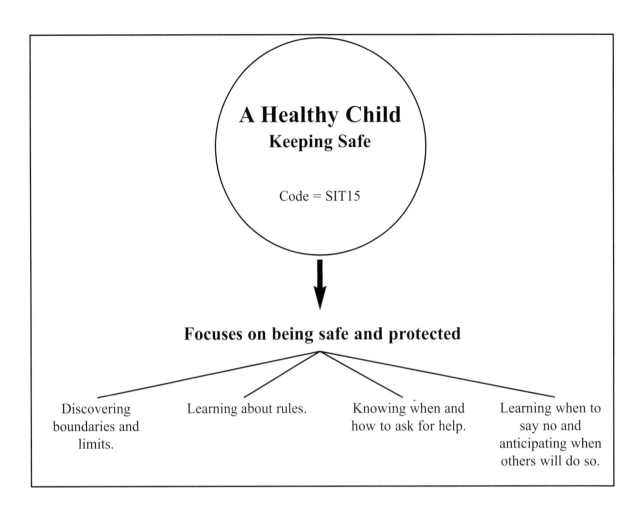

A Healthy Child
Keeping Safe

Code = SIT15

Focuses on being safe and protected

Discovering boundaries and limits.

Learning about rules.

Knowing when and how to ask for help.

Learning when to say no and anticipating when others will do so.

Development matters	Beginning to walk, climb and run with little sense of danger, babies focus on what they want.
Look, listen, note	Note the ways in which babies indicate what they need, including help from the adults.
Effective practice	Demonstrate clear and consistent boundaries and reasonable yet challenging expectations.
Play and practical support	Provide puppets, role-play materials, songs and rhymes which help babies and children focus on who they can trust. Let them know the importance of sharing their fears with an adult.

Sitters, Standers and Explorers

A Healthy Child
Keeping Safe

Development matters	Play and practical support
Beginning to walk, climb and run with little sense of danger, babies focus on what *they* want.	Provide puppets, role-play materials, songs and rhymes which help babies and children focus on who they can trust. Let them know the importance of sharing their fears with an adult.

Sample activity	Baby assault course challenge.
Resources	Gather together a selection of large play apparatus suitable for your age group, remembering to include items to walk around as well as climb over, crawl through and aim towards.
Health and safety	Ensure that challenges presented by the apparatus are commensurate with the babies' abilities.
Layout	Lay out a safe area on your carpet/matting with a clearly defined route from start to finish.
The role of the key worker	Guide each of your group of babies through the route in the manner best suited to their age/stage of development. Holding their hands or kneeling, go through the course backwards, so that they can come towards you throughout. Adapt the course for each child, but also with each pass, to take account of difficulties experienced or achievements made at the previous attempt. Provide encouragement throughout. Try encouraging other babies to sit and watch while they wait their turns, applauding at each successful pass.
Note	Note the ways in which babies indicate what they need, including help from the adults.
Questions to ask/ suggested interactions	• Can you duck down to go through this tunnel? • Now let's try to crawl over this little bridge . . . • Isn't Gabriel clever for stepping over that fence?
Comments	Remember to keep the assault course *very* basic, adjusting it for crawlers or walkers. Try to assist as little as possible, but remain aware so that where a baby holds out his hand to be held, you are there for him.

Sitters, Standers and Explorers

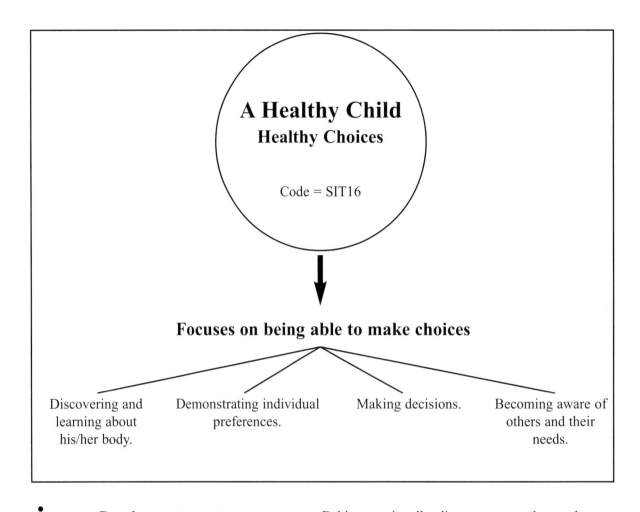

A Healthy Child
Healthy Choices

Code = SIT16

Focuses on being able to make choices

Discovering and learning about his/her body.

Demonstrating individual preferences.

Making decisions.

Becoming aware of others and their needs.

Development matters

Babies continually discover more about what they like and dislike.

Look, listen, note

Note how the environment (setting and adults) supports or might limit babies in expressing preferences and making choices.

Effective practice

Value and support the decisions children make and then go on to encourage them to try something else, recognising that one decision leads to another.

Play and practical support

Talk to children about the choices they have made and encourage them to find new areas to discover.

Sitters, Standers and Explorers

A Healthy Child
Healthy Choices

Development matters	Play and practical support
Babies continually discover more about what they like and dislike.	Talk to children about the choices they have made and encourage them to find new areas to discover.

Sample activity	Taste testing.
Resources	A selection of fresh fruit and vegetables of different textures suitable for the children in your group.
Health and safety	Ensure that foods are not on the exclusion list for this age group and that pieces are appropriate and do not present a risk of choking.
Layout	Set your table out so that you and your group can sit around the table with room to lay out plates so your group cannot reach. Cover each plate so the children can only see the plates one at a time.
The role of the key worker	Make your first selection something that the children are familiar with, and give them a piece to hold and taste. Observe their reactions, trying to put their expressions and reactions into words: 'You like that dont you?' or 'Was that not nice?' etc. Wait until each piece is eaten or discarded before introducing the next piece. Try to intersperse popular pieces with new tastes to encourage the babies to continue.
Note	Note how the environment (setting and adults) supports or might limit babies in expressing preferences and making choices.
Questions to ask/ suggested interactions	• Is that nice? • Does that feel crunchy? • Don't you like the tomato?
Comments	You could change this to be different types of food such as different bread – fresh, toasted, crusty, breadsticks etc. Don't forget to check that none of your group are wheat or gluten intolerant and that bread doesn't include nuts or seeds! Try to stick to five or six different tastes, repeating the exercise with the same fruit at intervals as baby's taste changes. Note down reactions to pass on to parents and other workers.

Sitters, Standers and Explorers

Case study

A day in the life of Tillie Mint, aged 14 months

Time	Activity	Achieved
8:00	Tilly arrives at nursery with her mum who passes over the terry towelling nappies. Tilly is happy to see her key worker, Sue, and waves goodbye to Mum easily. Sue helps Tilly build a house with the Mega Blocks.	SIT1 SIT13
8:45	As the babies move through into their own location Tilly is holding Sue's hand, but pulling her through, keen to get to her own room. Sue sits Tilly down at the table, encouraging her to choose her own bib and try to put it on herself, offering a helping hand.	SIT3 SIT15
9:00	Sheila brings in toast and jam for morning snack, and before the plates are ready Tilly is holding out her hand saying 'Ta' to Sarah who is nearest to the toast.	SIT8
9:30	While other staff tidy away the snack, Sue gets out the guitar that she has brought to nursery and Phil begins to play. Tilly is immediately interested in this and goes over to investigate. Phil shows her how to strum the strings and she is clearly impressed at the sounds she can make. Jeanette gets some more musical instruments out and before long most of the group has joined in. Tilly goes from one instrument to another while she tries them all out and ends up dancing for herself.	SIT5 SIT6 SIT9 SIT11
10:45	After a brief interlude with a different selection of toys, it is time for Tilly's group to visit the Sensory Room with another group. She walks down the corridor by herself, leading the way to get there quicker. Phil is by her side but Tilly prefers not to hold her hand and walk under her own steam. In the Sensory Room, Sue selects the projected images of under the sea and Tilly enjoys following the moving images across the floor for more than 10 minutes, but then instantly dismisses them and runs around the room shouting loudly to hear her own voice. She plays independently with different equipment but stops regularly to check that she is still being watched and laughs when she knows that she has somebody's attention.	SIT3 SIT6 SIT9 SIT11 SIT15
11:15	Session over, it is time to walk back to the room for a nappy change and to get ready for lunch. Tilly is not quite so anxious to return and lags behind the group, eventually sitting down on the floor in protest at having to leave. Sue picks her up with a laugh to soften her thunderous expression and Tilly soon softens. Taking her straight into the nappy change Sue can sense that Tilly is getting tired and will need livening up if she is to enjoy dinner and pudding before falling asleep. Sue tickles her tummy and makes her laugh while getting her changed.	SIT3 SIT10 SIT13 SIT16
11:30	Today's lunch is shepherd's pie with beetroot, which is brought in on plates to cool down. Again Tilly puts on her own bib and tries to get Phil's attention because she is nearest to the lunch. As soon as she has her plate in front of her, Tilly tucks in using her spoon and her fingers to push it on. When all of her group have their lunch Sue sits with them and asks if anybody would like her help. Asking Tilly directly, Tilly refuses to give Sue her spoon to help so Sue lets her get on with it. Watching her closely she offers more help as Tilly gets frustrated that she can't pick anything else up from the bowl. This time she lets Sue help her finish off her shepherd's pie. As her lunch bowl is collected by Jeanette, Tilly objects as Sue wipes her face and hand with a clean cloth in preparation for pudding which arrives almost instantly. Carrot cake is another of Tilly's favourites and she eats it very quickly.	SIT8 SIT11 SIT15

A day in the life of Tillie Mint, aged 14 months continued

Time	Activity	Achieved
12:10	After another wipe of her face and hands, Tilly is ready for her afternoon nap. Despite numerous attempts by Sue and other key staff, Tilly does not like to go to sleep on the floor cushions or in a cot. Instead she prefers to go to sleep in a buggy so Sue makes her comfortable, wheeling her up and down in the darkened room until she has dropped off. After a short while Tilly can be moved to a floor cushion where she will sleep longer than if she had stayed in the buggy. She is moved carefully, covered with her blanket and given her teddy to hug without her even batting an eyelid.	SIT14 SIT16
1:45	Tilly sleeps longer than normal today and wakes in a very good mood. For a little while she is happy playing with the large wooden toys that have been set out but soon spots a group of older children playing outside. Going over to the door she bangs loudly, saying 'Out! Out!' to anybody who will listen.	SIT2 SIT8
2:00	Phil brings in a small pile of coats belonging to the older babies and asks Tilly which is her coat. Tilly immediately identifies her coat and gives it to Phil to put on. As soon as her coat is on she stands impatiently at the door again shouting 'Out!' while she waits for the others in her group to have their coats put on. Door opens and she is raring to go. While outside she plays football, runs up and down the patio a great deal and bangs on the windows of other rooms to attract the attention of other children.	SIT4 SIT10 SIT11
2:30	Back inside she is ready for something calm so Phil asks her group, 'Would you like a story?' Although she is not in Phil's group Tilly simply takes a seat with the group and enjoys *My Jungle* with the other group. Tilly thoroughly enjoys the book, making verbal comments about the pop-up animals and bright pictures. She remains sitting still while the book is read again, joining in slightly more than the first reading. After this Phil encourages the children to sit with their own books and they all sit happily and read the board books that they are given.	SIT4 SIT10 SIT11
3:00	Time for afternoon snack and Sheila has arrived with cheese and crackers. Without any instruction Tilly goes over to the table but finds no chairs. Instinctively she goes over to the milk kitchen and bangs at Sue, who she can see through the window. Sue gets the message and helps Tilly to put a chair at the table, asking her: 'Where shall I put it? Do you want to sit by Andrew?' Tilly indicates where she would like to sit by pointing next to Jack and sits on the chair immediately. She enjoys her snack, needing no help at all, and almost helping Jack to finish off his before he spots her.	SIT11 SIT15
3:30	After snack time there is a selection of coloured pencils and coloured paper laid out on the tables and Duplo on the floor. Tilly selects a handful of pencils and makes her marks on the paper with all of the pencils at the same time. Looking at her picture she is clearly pleased with her result and gathers a handful of pencils in the other hand too, making her marks on the paper with both hands at the same time. She gets fed up very quickly and drops the pencils, watching as some of them roll off the table and onto the floor. She sits playing with the Duplo, building a tower with Sue until her mum and dad arrive at 4:00.	SIT10 SIT12
4:00	Sitting playing happily, for a minute or two Tilly is unaware that her parents have arrived. Sue smiles to them but does not draw Tilly's attention to them so that they can watch her play for a while. As soon as they are spotted any building plans are forgotten and she runs as far away as possible so that Dad has to chase her to put her coat on. This gives Mum a chance to ask Sue about her day, and Sue gives her lots of feedback before they leave for the afternoon.	SIT4

Code list	Additional suggestions
A Strong Child	
SIT1 Me, Myself and I	Whose coat is this? Who has red shoes?
SIT2 Being Acknowledged and Affirmed	Roll call – who's in today?; Sharing nursery with Mum/Dad.
SIT3 Developing Self-assurance	Clever things I can do; Helping others.
SIT4 A Sense of Belonging	Sharing a group hug; Doing things together.
A Skilful Communicator	
SIT5 Being Together	Chatting together with friends; Shredded paper play with a friend.
SIT6 Finding a Voice	Tell me what you'd like to do next; Question time.
SIT7 Listening and Responding	Taking turns for the first time; What are we going to do next?
SIT8 Making Meaning	You tell *me* what to do next; Choosing which story to listen to.
A Competent Learner	
SIT9 Making Connections	Cardboard box play; What can we find in our garden?
SIT10 Being Imaginative	Heuristic play session; Down on the farm.
SIT11 Being Creative	What happens if you watch *me* paint?; Playing the piano together.
SIT12 Representing	Printing with things around us; Building without bricks.
A Healthy Child	
SIT13 Emotional Well-being	These are a few of my favourite things; Sharing my favourite person.
SIT14 Growing and Developing	Music and movement; Learning to use my spoon and fork.
SIT15 Keeping Safe	Putting on my shoes; Getting to know a new friend.
SIT16 Healthy Choices	Learning to share my toys; Getting dressed to play outside.

Aspect title:	
Component title:	**Code =**

Development matters	Play and practical support

Sample activity	
Resources	
Health and safety	
Layout	
The role of the key worker	
Note	
Questions to ask/ suggested interactions	• •
Comments	

(P)　　　　　　　　　　　　**Sitters, Standers and Explorers**

Completed by:　　　　　　　　　　　　　　　　**Date:**

Aspect title:	
Component title:	**Code =**

Development matters	Play and practical support

Sample activity	
Resources	
Health and safety	
Layout	
The role of the key worker	
Note	
Questions to ask/ suggested interactions	• •
Comments	

(P)   **Sitters, Standers and Explorers**

Completed by: **Date:**

Sitters, Standers and Explorers
(8–18 months)

Date of activity:	Supervised by:
Children involved:	
Comments	

Date of activity:	Supervised by:
Children involved:	
Comments	

Date of activity:	Supervised by:
Children involved:	
Comments	

(P)

Movers, Shakers
and
Players

(18–24 months)

Movers, Shakers and Players
(18–24 months)

Section index

Notes for this section

What can one say about this age group that you don't already know? This is a very busy and active group, still guided under a ratio of three children per member of staff. Here we will be busy introducing potty/toilet training and encouraging greater personal independence. Many of our activity sessions might be interrupted by sudden dashes to the toilet and, of course, there is an increase in temper tantrums that might also interrupt our sessions. So what do we do about this? Think sensibly. You will know the children in your group and the likelihood of one or both of those interruptions so plan accordingly. Utilise extra pairs of hands in the group, including volunteers or apprentices to step in and temporarily remove a child having a temper, or intervene in a dispute. This means that the worker leading the activity will not need to be too distracted and the other children can still benefit from the full activity.

If an extra pair of hands is not available consider joining together with another group of similar ability children and agree with their key worker who will lead and who will support the activity.

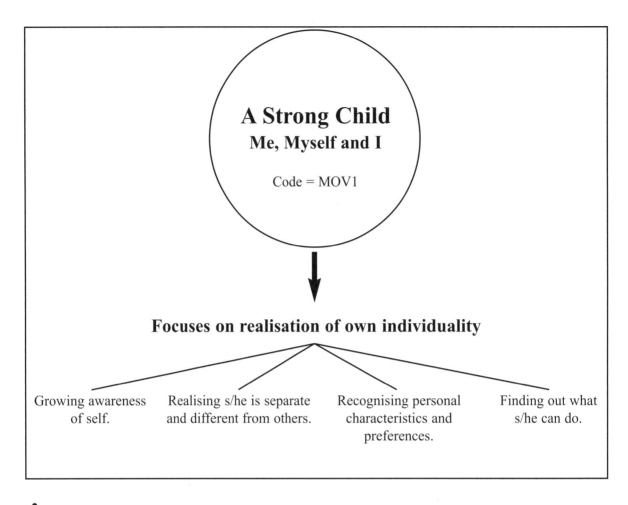

A Strong Child
Me, Myself and I

Code = MOV1

Focuses on realisation of own individuality

Growing awareness of self.

Realising s/he is separate and different from others.

Recognising personal characteristics and preferences.

Finding out what s/he can do.

Development matters	Young children learn they have similarities and differences that connect them to, and distinguish them from, others.
Look, listen, note	Note how, with your support and encouragement, young children begin to make decisions and develop preferences, thereby beginning to establish their autonomy.
Effective practice	Recognising, accepting and understanding that carrying, sucking or playing with something such as a dummy that they have brought from home helps young children as they move between home and a new setting.
Play and practical support	Value young children's comfort objects and show them that you understand that they meet their emotional needs.

Movers, Shakers and Players

A Strong Child
Me, Myself and I

Code = MOV1

Development matters	Play and practical support
Young children learn they have similarities and differences that connect them to, and distinguish them from, others.	Value young children's comfort objects and show them that you understand that they meet their emotional needs.

Sample activity	What's my favourite thing?
Resources	Ensure that each of the children present have their comforter with them if it is present in nursery on the day.
Health and safety	There are no health and safety risks to this activity.
Layout	Sit in a circle.
The role of the key worker	Talk to all of the children about things that we all have, such as two feet, two hands, two eyes etc. and encourage them to point at the appropriate thing. Move on to things that we have in common but are different, such as different shoes on our feet, different coloured eyes etc. Then point out that we all have a favourite thing, taking care to point out that not all of us want to bring our favourite thing to nursery if this is case. Point out that these 'same but different' things are another thing we have in common and talk about the benefits of the favourite things from your group, e.g. Oliver loves his blanket because it's all warm and snugly, while Joel loves his silky because it reminds him of Mum and helps him not to miss her too much until she comes back.
Note	Note how, with your support and encouragement, young children begin to make decisions and develop preferences, thereby beginning to establish their autonomy.
Questions to ask/ suggested interactions	• Who has two hands? • Who has shoes on their feet? • Who has curly hair?
Comments	Don't forget to include dummies, teddies or other things that come to nursery intermittently, as well as identifying what your own favourite thing is.

Movers, Shakers and Players

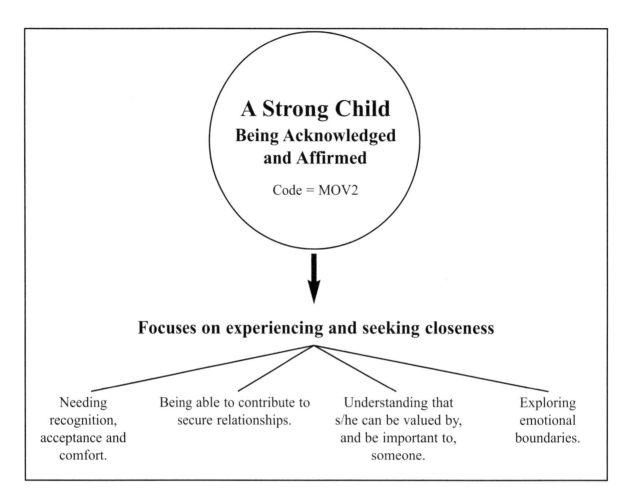

A Strong Child
Being Acknowledged and Affirmed

Code = MOV2

Focuses on experiencing and seeking closeness

| Needing recognition, acceptance and comfort. | Being able to contribute to secure relationships. | Understanding that s/he can be valued by, and be important to, someone. | Exploring emotional boundaries. |

Development matters

Young children strive for responses from others which confirm, contribute to, or challenge their understanding of themselves.

Look, listen, note

Note when, where, how and why you praise and appreciate young children and how they respond.

Effective practice

Tell, as well as read stories, looking at and interacting with young children as a way of letting them know that you think they are important and valued.

Play and practical support

Use different voices to tell stories and get young children to join in wherever possible, sometimes using puppets, soft toys or real objects as props.

Movers, Shakers and Players

A Strong Child
Being Acknowledged and Affirmed

Code = MOV2

Development matters	Play and practical support
Young children strive for responses from others which confirm, contribute to, or challenge their understanding of themselves.	Use different voices to tell stories and get young children to join in wherever possible, sometimes using puppets, soft toys or real objects as props.

Sample activity	Puppet theatre.
Resources	A small selection of thematic puppets and a familiar story like *The Three Little Pigs*.
Health and safety	Ensure that puppets selected are appropriate to this age group.
Layout	Sit together at circle time, puppets laid out in front of you.
The role of the key worker	When the children are seated, ask them if they know which story the puppets want to tell. Picking up the main character, tell the children that you are going to be the wolf and ask who would like to be the first little pig. Encourage the children to stay seated, but give out the puppets to the children around the group. Take the role of storyteller as well as the wolf and encourage the children with puppets to act out the story, while the other children join in on the repetitive chants such as 'I'll huff, and I'll puff...' etc.
Note	Note when, where, how and why you praise and appreciate young children and how they respond.
Questions to ask/ suggested interactions	• Who can remember what the pigs say when the wolf knocks on their doors? • And what does the wolf say he'll do next? • Do you think the pigs are scared?
Comments	Remember to include all of the children, even those who did not want to participate by holding the puppets. Remember to offer other children the chance to be a puppeteer next time; they may not want to volunteer themselves. Try to vary the stories but keep to a small, familiar selection.

Movers, Shakers and Players

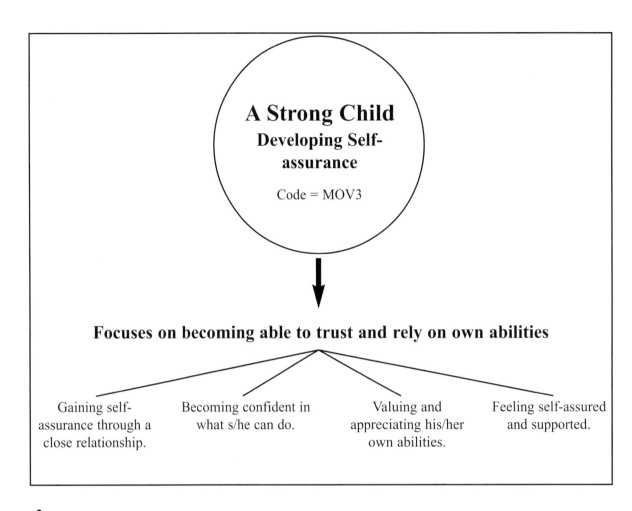

A Strong Child
Developing Self-assurance

Code = MOV3

Focuses on becoming able to trust and rely on own abilities

| Gaining self-assurance through a close relationship. | Becoming confident in what s/he can do. | Valuing and appreciating his/her own abilities. | Feeling self-assured and supported. |

Development matters

Young children explore what they can do on their own, if given support.

Look, listen, note

Note how you prepare for and resource playful activities for young children to engage in independently.

Effective practice

Encourage young children to be part of collaborative activities, making sure they are not always dependent upon your presence for them to contribute and participate.

Play and practical support

Collaborative games and communal sharing times encourage a young child to take more responsibility.

Movers, Shakers and Players

A Strong Child
Developing Self-assurance

Code = MOV3

Development matters	Play and practical support
Young children explore what they can do on their own, if given support.	Collaborative games and communal sharing times encourage a young child to take more responsibility.

Sample activity	'I am the music man'.
Resources	A selection of musical instruments so that each child participating has a different piece. It may help for you to have one of each in front of you to use alongside the children.
Health and safety	Ensure that musical instruments used are appropriate to the children's ages.
Layout	Sit in a circle with the musical instruments in front of each participant.
The role of the key worker	Sing the tune and encourage all of the children to join in without using their instruments. When it comes to naming the first instrument, choose the instrument that you have given to the first child on your left. Invite him (and only him if you can) to join in with that section of the song while all of the other children sing. If the child is nervous or unsure, pick up your instrument and encourage him to play along with you. Move around the circle in this way until all of the children have had a go on their own, encouraging them to place their instrument on the floor in front of them when it is not their turn. As the last child in the group has completed her turn, make the last verse for a full orchestra and encourage everybody to join in.
Note	Note how you prepare for and resource playful activities for young children to engage in independently.
Questions to ask/ suggested interactions	• Who might be next? • Who has the tambourine? • Can we all clap our hands while John beats his drum?
Comments	Remember to keep this group of children small so that it does not seem like forever that the children have instruments, but must leave them on the floor. Finish the session with a big parade around the room/carpet playing our instruments as loudly as we can.

Movers, Shakers and Players

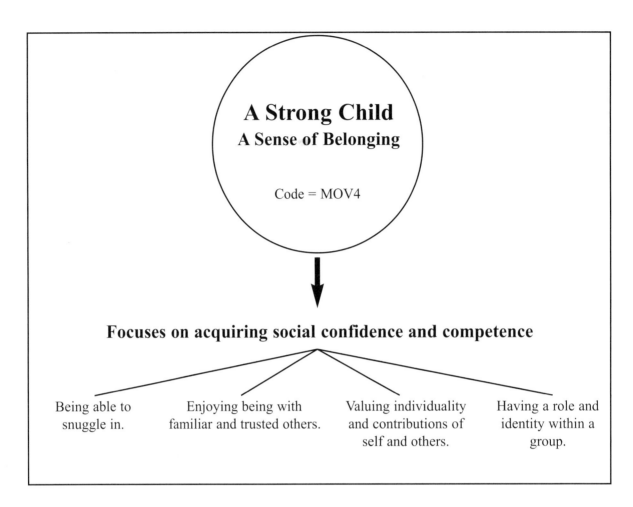

A Strong Child
A Sense of Belonging

Code = MOV4

Focuses on acquiring social confidence and competence

| Being able to snuggle in. | Enjoying being with familiar and trusted others. | Valuing individuality and contributions of self and others. | Having a role and identity within a group. |

Development matters

Young children's developing attitudes and beliefs are shaped by the value that others place on individual differences and similarities.

Look, listen, note

Note young children's questions about difference, e.g. skin colour, hair, friends.

Effective practice

Find ways to value and celebrate each young child within the group by making routines such as feeding and changing personal.

Play and practical support

Create opportunities for young children to be involved in the domestic routines that link home and the out-of-home setting, being mindful of ways in which these may differ culturally.

Movers, Shakers and Players

A Strong Child

A Sense of Belonging

Code = MOV4

Development matters	Play and practical support
Young children's developing attitudes and beliefs are shaped by the value that others place on individual differences and similarities.	Create opportunities for young children to be involved in the domestic routines that link home and the out-of-home setting, being mindful of ways in which these may differ culturally.

Sample activity	Nursery salon.
Resources	A selection of hairdressing equipment such as brushes, combs, hairdryers and mirrors as well as hair colour charts, salon gowns etc.
Health and safety	Ensure that brushes etc. are regularly sterilised. Bottles should be washed thoroughly to remove all trace of the original product. Hairdryers should have the flex removed and mirrors be unbreakable.
Layout	Set out a few chairs for 'clients', mirrors for the 'stylists' to look into and a waiting area, but don't expect too much patience!
The role of the key worker	Encourage the children to talk about who it is that helps them get their hair ready for nursery in the morning. Encourage them to talk about what Mum/Dad etc. does with their hair, role playing it on another child. Children whose hair needs nothing or little done to it before nursery should be encouraged to consider why. A shaved head clearly doesn't need brushing, but might need more trips to the hairdresser's than somebody with long, curly hair. Compare hair colours to the charts and discuss the differences in the group.
Note	Note young children's questions about differences, e.g. skin colour, hair, friends.
Questions to ask/ suggested interactions	• Who helps you get ready for nursery in the morning? • What do they need to do to get your hair ready? • Do they do the same to their own hair?
Comments	Of course, your comments here will differ depending on the group, but you might need to make a note to gather together different resources next time. Clippers or oils might need to be improvised, or scarves gathered together to finish off the hair.

Movers, Shakers and Players

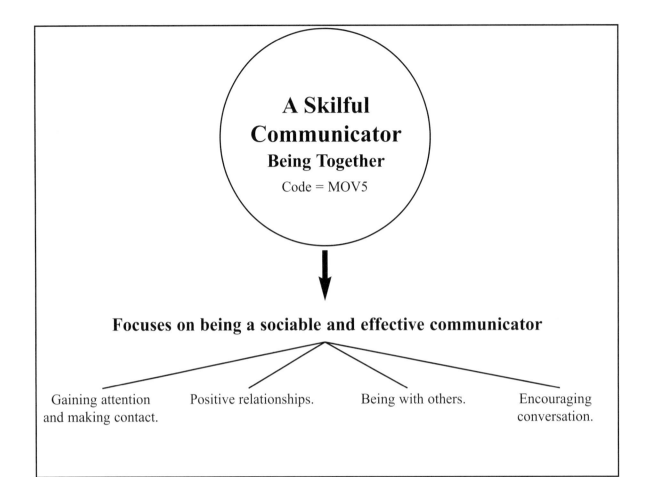

A Skilful
Communicator
Being Together
Code = MOV5

Focuses on being a sociable and effective communicator

Gaining attention
and making contact.

Positive relationships.

Being with others.

Encouraging
conversation.

Development matters	Young children form friendships and can be caring towards each other.
Look, listen, note	Note how adults and other children respond, e.g. mirroring, echoing, interpreting and sharing objects.
Effective practice	Help children learn the names of other children and important people in their lives, e.g. through songs and rhymes.
Play and practical support	Spend time with young children sharing photographs, either in books or placed where they can be seen, e.g. on skirting boards or mobiles, showing family, friends, favourite foods or pets.

Movers, Shakers and Players

A Skilful Communicator
Being Together

Code = MOV5

Development matters	Play and practical support
Young children form friendships and can be caring towards each other.	Spend time with young children sharing photographs, either in books or placed where they can be seen, e.g. on skirting boards or mobiles, showing family, friends, favourite foods or pets.

Sample activity	'My family and other animals'.
Resources	Ask Mum or Dad to bring in a selection of photographs of family members, pets, favourite places etc. for each of your group. Ensure that they make notes on the back of each photo of who/where etc.
Health and safety	There are no health and safety risks to this activity.
Layout	Sitting with your group in a close circle but around the table.
The role of the key worker	Select one child from your group each time that you schedule this activity and start the discussion by asking the particular child: 'Who is this?' and encourage him to tell the rest of the group about the people in the photograph. Use the notes from the photographs and your own knowledge of the family to prompt. Encourage others to tell the group about their own aunt or their own pet, or even their holiday in Florida, but remember that this session is about one child so return to this child and his photographs quite regularly. Finish the session with a group hug so that everybody feels valued.
Note	Note how adults and other children respond, e.g. mirroring, echoing, interpreting and sharing objects.
Questions to ask/ suggested interactions	• Does anybody else have an Aunty Jean? • Who can guess what Jack's pet fish is called? • Does it look like Jack is enjoying his holiday?
Comments	Try to pick the more demonstrative of your group to share this session first, encouraging them to share their photographs with others. Hopefully, when it is somebody else's turn they may be more likely to share.

Movers, Shakers and Players

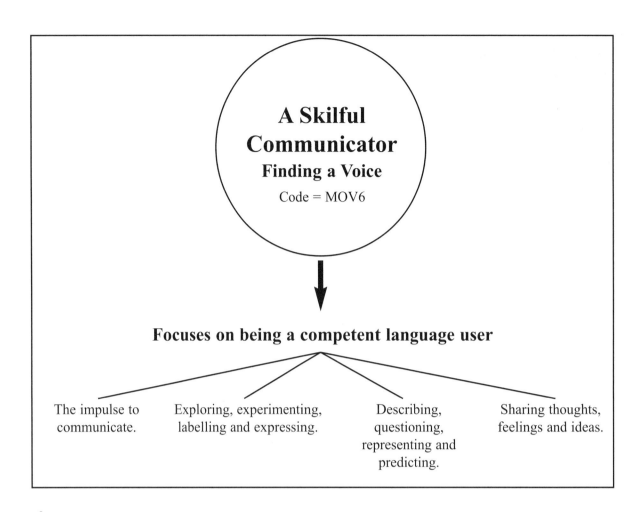

A Skilful Communicator

Finding a Voice

Code = MOV6

Focuses on being a competent language user

The impulse to communicate.

Exploring, experimenting, labelling and expressing.

Describing, questioning, representing and predicting.

Sharing thoughts, feelings and ideas.

Development matters	Young children use single-word and two-word utterances to convey simple and more complex messages.
Look, listen, note	Note the meanings young children generate in their language through the creative ways in which they combine words.
Effective practice	Recognise young children's competence and appreciate their efforts when they show their understanding of new words and phrases.
Play and practical support	Provide everyday objects found in the home, e.g. a sponge, soft nail brush, plastic pan scrub for babies and children to explore, investigate and talk about.

Movers, Shakers and Players

A Skilful Communicator
Finding a Voice

Code = MOV6

Development matters	Play and practical support
Young children use single-word and two-word utterances to convey simple and more complex messages.	Provide everyday objects found in the home, e.g. a sponge, soft nail brush and plastic pan scrub for babies and children to explore, investigate and talk about.

Sample activity	What is it and what is it for?
Resources	Gather together a selection of items from home for a similar purpose, such as a sponge, face cloth, toothbrush and towel.
Health and safety	Ensure that items selected are new or freshly washed.
Layout	Sit together in a circle.
The role of the key worker	Start this session by selecting the most familiar item and pass it around the group to handle. Ask the children: 'What is it?' When they have identified what it is, ask the children to say what it is for. Encourage miming of the use, but also a verbal description of it. Ask individual children: 'What is this for Shabanna?', occasionally encouraging them to tell you rather than show you. When they respond 'brush teeth' praise their input, and repeat it in a longer sentence: 'Yes, that's right, we brush our teeth to keep them clean.'
Note	Note the meanings young children generate in their language through the creative ways in which they combine words.
Questions to ask/ suggested interactions	• What is this? • What does it do? • How do we use it?
Comments	Use different collections of items to expand the children's use of words in very simple early sentences. Try kitchen items, clothing, writing implements etc.

A Skilful Communicator
Listening and Responding

Code = MOV7

Focuses on listening and responding appropriately to the language of others

| Listening and paying attention to what others say. | Making playful and serious responses. | Enjoying and sharing stories, songs, rhymes and games. | Learning about words and meanings. |

Development matters

Young children are able to respond to simple requests and grasp meaning from context or situation.

Look, listen, note

Different kinds of activities encourage young children to listen and respond. Observe young children's reactions in play, to music, story, rhymes, TV and computer activities.

Effective practice

Be available to explore and talk about things that interest young children indoors and outdoors, and listen to and respond to their questions, both serious and playful.

Play and practical support

Use puppets and other props to encourage listening and responding, e.g. when singing a familiar song, asking questions, joining in young children's play. Encourage repetition.

Movers, Shakers and Players

A Skilful Communicator
Listening and Responding

Development matters	Play and practical support
Young children are able to respond to simple requests and grasp meaning from context or situation.	Use puppets and other props to encourage listening and responding, e.g. when singing a familiar song, asking questions, joining in young children's play. Encourage repetition.

Sample activity	Simon says . . .
Resources	Whatever is at hand.
Health and safety	There are no health and safety risks to this activity.
Layout	Stand together in a circle.
The role of the key worker	With this group of young children, keep your actions simple but clear. Start out by joining in with your action requests such as: 'Simon says put your hands on your head' or 'Simon says sit down on the floor.' When you are sure all of the children are listening and responding, stop doing the actions yourself and encourage the children to think for themselves. Towards the end of your session make your suggestions silly or fun, to reward the children's participation.
Note	Different kinds of activities encourage young children to listen and respond. Observe young children's reactions in play, to music, story, rhymes, TV and computer activities.
Questions to ask/ suggested interactions	• Simon says put your hands on your head and jump up and down. • Simon says sit down with your legs crossed. • Put on a silly hat.
Comments	At this early stage you should not expect the children to differentiate between the instruction preceded by: 'Simon says' and the one that isn't.

Movers, Shakers and Players

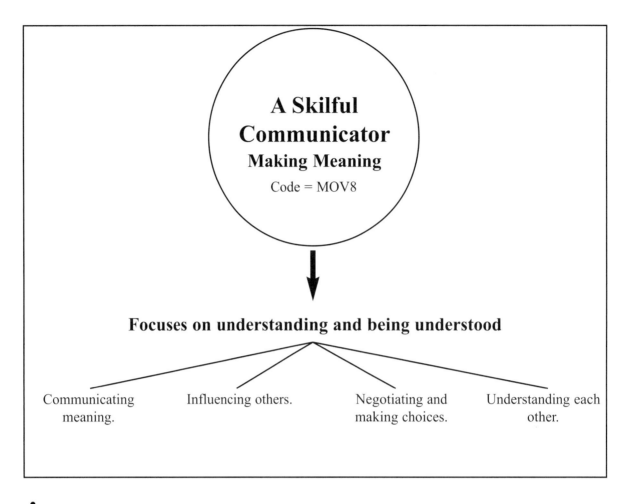

A Skilful Communicator
Making Meaning
Code = MOV8

Focuses on understanding and being understood

Communicating meaning.

Influencing others.

Negotiating and making choices.

Understanding each other.

Development matters	Young children use actions and words to make and justify choices and influence the behaviour and responses of others.
Look, listen, note	Note the ways in which young children negotiate with adults and other children and the circumstances in which this takes place.
Effective practice	Respect young children's choices and encourage their growing ability to negotiate and bargain with you.
Play and practical support	Display and discuss photographs with young children that convey specific messages, e.g. a child in conflict with an adult, taking on a role, choosing a biscuit.

Movers, Shakers and Players

A Skilful Communicator
Making Meaning

Code = MOV8

Development matters	Play and practical support
Young children use actions and words to make and justify choices and influence the behaviour and responses of others.	Display and discuss photographs with young children that convey specific messages, e.g. a child in conflict with an adult, taking on a role, choosing a biscuit.

Sample activity	What shall we wear to go here?
Resources	A selection of enlarged photographs showing different climates or weather conditions. A selection of clothing to suit the photographs prepared, including sun hats, sunscreen, Wellington boots, gloves etc.
Health and safety	Ensure that sunscreen bottles are properly rinsed and the use of laces, ties etc. are properly supervised.
Layout	Try to lay the items out so that they are grouped together – gloves, summer hats, winter hats etc. Leave plenty of space for the children to move around in.
The role of the key worker	Sit with the children in a circle and talk to them about the weather today and the clothes they have put on. Show the first photograph and ask the children to talk about what they see. Is it hot, cold, wet? After reaching a general consensus about the appropriate clothing, ask the children to select some things from the display to put on. Sit the children down again and discuss another photograph, encouraging the children to choose items that are appropriate. Make two or three changes of weather before leaving the children to play with the clothes unprompted for the rest of the session.
Note	Note the ways in which young children negotiate with adults and other children and the circumstances in which this takes place.
Questions to ask/ suggested interactions	• The sun is shining but there is snow on the ground – what should we choose to keep our feet dry and warm? • What kind of hat would we need to keep our ears warm in this wind?
Comments	Don't forget that you may need to help children put some things on or take others off. You will also need to provide a good selection of each item to fit the size of your group. Older children might take to this activity quickly, requiring less prompting before selecting the right clothing.

Movers, Shakers and Players

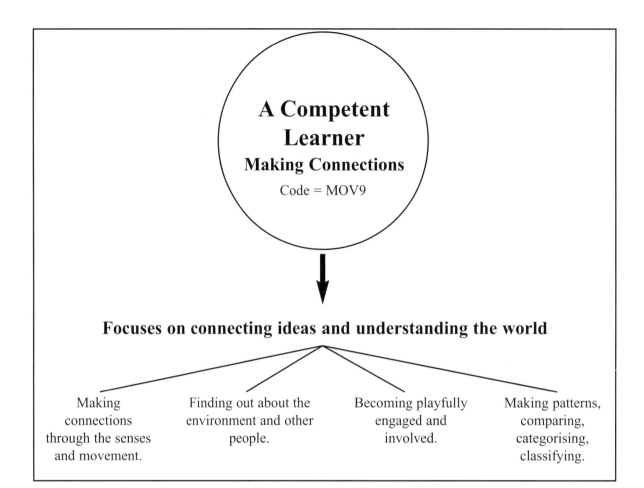

A Competent Learner
Making Connections
Code = MOV9

Focuses on connecting ideas and understanding the world

| Making connections through the senses and movement. | Finding out about the environment and other people. | Becoming playfully engaged and involved. | Making patterns, comparing, categorising, classifying. |

Development matters   Young children learn through repeating patterns of play, sometimes called 'schema' (see the *Birth to three matters* CD-ROM).

Look, listen, note   Note connections in young children's movements and activities, e.g. how they paint in circles, run in circles.

Effective practice   Provide stimulating materials for young children to match, sort, classify and categorise, e.g. shades of paint to their skin colour, sorting and counting animals during play with a farmyard or zoo.

Play and practical support   Make a diary of photographs with a young child to record an important occasion, e.g. finding a worm or visiting a special place.

Movers, Shakers and Players

A Competent Learner
Making Connections

Code = MOV9

Development matters	Play and practical support
Young children learn through repeating patterns of play, sometimes called 'schema' (you can find out more about this on the *Birth to three matters* CD-ROM).	Make a diary of photographs with a young child to record an important occasion, e.g. finding a worm in the garden or visiting a special place.

Sample activity	What happens next?
Resources	A Polaroid or digital camera where possible, or a speedy developer nearby.
Health and safety	There are no health and safety risks to this activity.
Layout	The same layout and routine that happens on most normal days in your room.
The role of the key worker	Talking through the day's activities is an important part of encouraging children to come to terms with their day in nursery and helps to form the skills required to predict. Use language that encourages the children to think about what they are doing now in relation to what happens next. Think about how you start your day. At one nursery the children all start together in one room, moving into the next at the same time every day. Take a photograph of the children moving from one room to the next and of what they will do when they get there (put the chairs around the tables ready for snack). Follow this throughout the day, taking photographs of what happens next on each occasion. Once developed, use this collection of photographs to talk about the day out of context, rather than what they really will do next.
Note	Note connections in young children's movements and activities, e.g. how they paint in circles, run in circles.
Questions to ask/ suggested interactions	• What do we do after snack time? • Then what happens? • Where do we go before our mums come to collect us?
Comments	Although they may be unfamiliar with the language used, you will find that children in this group have already developed a clear mind map of the routine of their day. Encourage them to talk about other issues they have in relation to this routine, e.g. first we will have a nap after lunch, then we'll play in the garden, then have snack and *then* Mum will come!

Movers, Shakers and Players

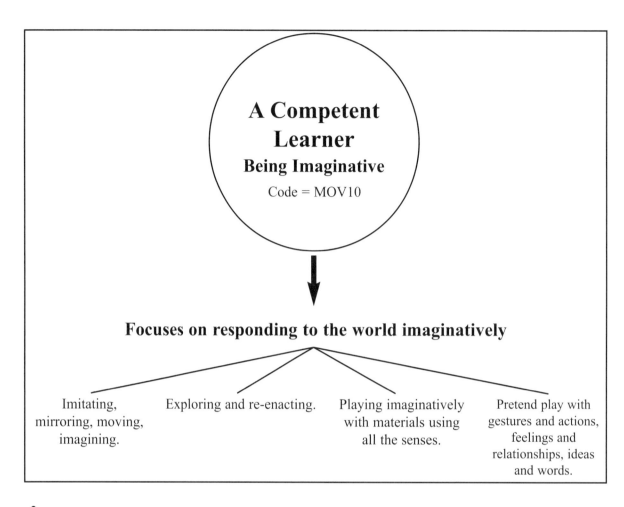

A Competent
Learner
Being Imaginative
Code = MOV10

Focuses on responding to the world imaginatively

Imitating, mirroring, moving, imagining.

Exploring and re-enacting.

Playing imaginatively with materials using all the senses.

Pretend play with gestures and actions, feelings and relationships, ideas and words.

Development matters	Young children re-enact familiar scenes with the help of people, props and resources.
Look, listen, note	Look at the kinds of props and materials that young children use imaginatively – note anything you might add.
Effective practice	Provide resources that support young children's imaginative learning, e.g. hats, scarves, boxes, materials.
Play and practical support	Young children enjoy playing with real things. Telephones, pans and brushes provide a link with home and lead to imitative and imaginative play.

Movers, Shakers and Players

A Competent Learner
Being Imaginative

Code = MOV10

Development matters	Play and practical support
Young children re-enact familiar scenes with the help of people, props and resources.	Young children enjoy playing with real things. Telephones, pans and brushes provide a link with home and lead to imitative and imaginative play.

Sample activity	Role play in the home corner.
Resources	A selection of real props to make the home corner realistic. Provide equipment from a variety of cultural settings to ensure that all children having something familiar as well as something to explore.
Health and safety	Care should be taken to ensure that all items included present no risks to children in unsupervised play.
Layout	A home space that is clearly defined, ensuring that a real sense of privacy can be achieved wherever possible.
The role of the key worker	The hardest part about role play for the key worker is being close enough to observe without intruding, yet being near enough to offer support if requested. Watch carefully to ensure that any intervention on your behalf is *really* necessary. Aim to keep your participation to a minimum.
Note	Look at the kinds of props and materials young children use imaginatively – note anything you might add.
Questions to ask/ suggested interactions	• Try not to ask any questions during the activity, but there may be questions prompted by the things you observed.
Comments	Take care to provide a realistic selection of equipment for this activity. Pots and pans and other cooking utensils may be borrowed from homes if necessary.

Movers, Shakers and Players

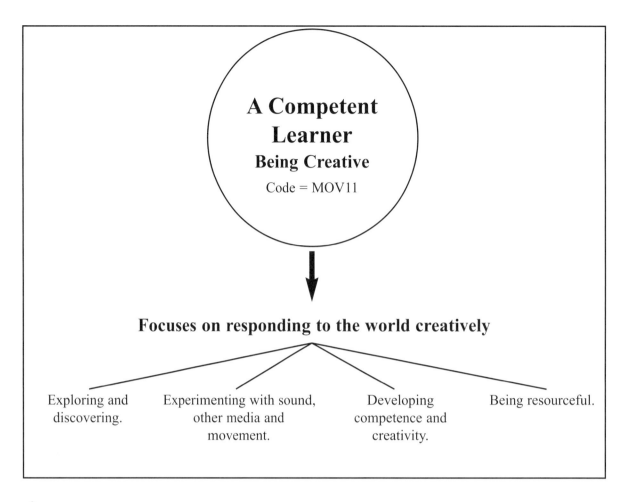

A Competent Learner

Being Creative

Code = MOV11

Focuses on responding to the world creatively

Exploring and discovering.

Experimenting with sound, other media and movement.

Developing competence and creativity.

Being resourceful.

Development matters	As young children become more mobile they express themselves through physical action and sound.
Look, listen, note	Observe how young children create new situations in their play, e.g. combining materials such as sand and water and transporting them from one area to another.
Effective practice	Encourage independence as young children explore particular patterns of thoughts or movement, sometimes referred to as 'schemas'.
Play and practical support	Even the youngest children can, with support, relish playing with sand (both damp and dry), water and playdough.

Movers, Shakers and Players

A Competent Learner
Being Creative

Code = MOV11

Development matters	Play and practical support
As young children become more mobile they express themselves through physical action and sound.	Even the youngest child can, with support, relish playing with sand (both damp and dry), water and playdough.

Sample activity	A day at the beach in the sand tray.
Resources	A selection of Duplo, Playmobil or other small world people and pets. A sand tray with half sand and a shallow end of water for the sea.
Health and safety	The same care should be taken as in any sand activity.
Layout	Before the children join the activity, set the sand out with families sunbathing, children making sandcastles and others in the water.
The role of the key worker	Encourage the children to talk about what they can see and then take a step back while they perhaps relive a day of their own at the beach. While observing, try to throw in occasional pieces of food for thought, such as what might happen if the tide came in (you could add more water), or what might happen if the wind became strong (you could blow the water into the sand). Encourage the children to explore the thought of waves crashing onto the beach, or a dog splashing about in the water and into sandcastles.
Note	Observe how young children create new situations in their play, e.g. combining materials such as sand and water and transporting them from one area to another.
Questions to ask/ suggested interactions	• What might happen to that boy playing near to the edge if the tide comes in? • What might those people do to cool down if they get all hot?
Comments	Try different scenes such as dinosaurs in a prehistoric landscape or tractors on a building site. Introducing familiar equipment in an unfamiliar way will encourage children to see other things that might be added for extra enjoyment. Try not to say 'no' unless the piece will be destroyed by play in this manner.

Movers, Shakers and Players

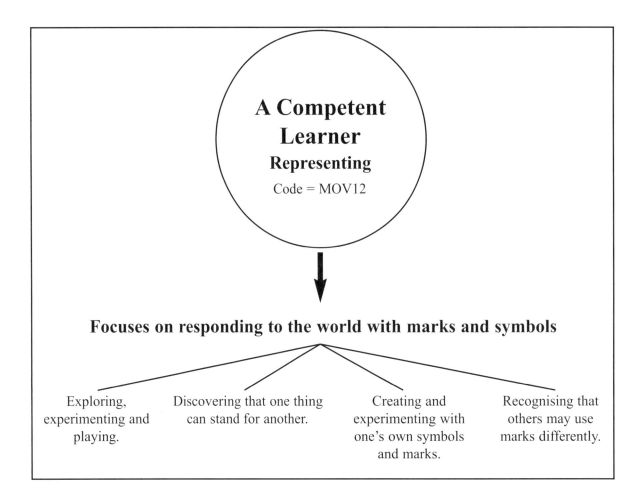

A Competent Learner
Representing
Code = MOV12

Focuses on responding to the world with marks and symbols

Exploring, experimenting and playing.

Discovering that one thing can stand for another.

Creating and experimenting with one's own symbols and marks.

Recognising that others may use marks differently.

Development matters	As young children explore tools and materials they make marks to which they give meaning.
Look, listen, note	Note examples of young children using one thing to stand for another, e.g. a box for a car.
Effective practice	Give young children who are keen to represent the same experience repeatedly a range of mark-making materials.
Play and practical support	Discuss with young children what their marks represent and help them to understand that print carries meaning.

Movers, Shakers and Players

A Competent Learner
Representing

Development matters	Play and practical support
As young children explore tools and materials they make marks to which they give meaning.	Discuss with young children what their marks represent and help them to understand that print carries meaning.

Sample activity	Free painting session outside.
Resources	A selection of paint pots containing very watery paint with big chunky brushes. Big aprons over warm coats.
Health and safety	The same care should be taken to ensure that the outdoor environment is safe as in usual outdoor play activities.
Layout	Clear a large space on a cemented area of the garden or use a large blank wall.
The role of the key worker	Encourage each child in your group to select two or three pots of paint that they might like to paint with, and ask each of them to draw a picture of themselves playing on their favourite bike. Ensure that each child has a clearly identified section of the wall and try not to interrupt until each child stands back to appreciate their work. Without saying 'What's that?' encourage each child to tell you about their painting. Listen carefully so that you do not ask what 'this is' when the child may just have finished explaining in their own words. When possible allow the art work to dry before letting anybody else play outside so that the art work can be enjoyed by all. Remember that you may need to wash the paintings away before starting another session if there has been no rain.
Note	Observe early marks that young children make when given a crayon or brush.
Questions to ask/ suggested interactions	• Tell me about the red parts of your picture. • Would you like me to swap a colour with somebody else?
Comments	In hot weather this activity can be enjoyed without paint, just by using cold water. The children can change their drawings simply by letting the sun heat the surface and dry up the water.

Movers, Shakers and Players

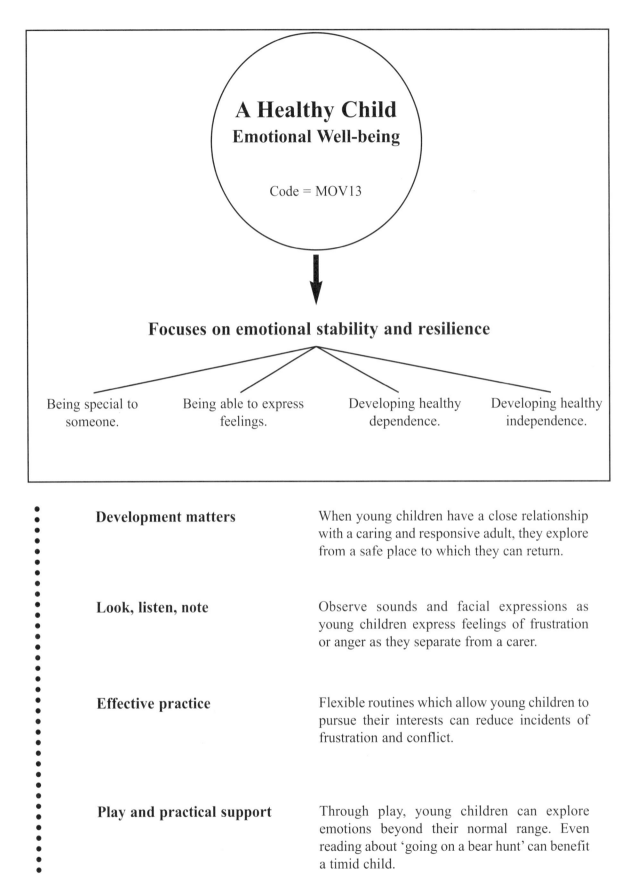

A Healthy Child
Emotional Well-being

Code = MOV13

Focuses on emotional stability and resilience

Being special to someone.

Being able to express feelings.

Developing healthy dependence.

Developing healthy independence.

Development matters

When young children have a close relationship with a caring and responsive adult, they explore from a safe place to which they can return.

Look, listen, note

Observe sounds and facial expressions as young children express feelings of frustration or anger as they separate from a carer.

Effective practice

Flexible routines which allow young children to pursue their interests can reduce incidents of frustration and conflict.

Play and practical support

Through play, young children can explore emotions beyond their normal range. Even reading about 'going on a bear hunt' can benefit a timid child.

Movers, Shakers and Players

A Healthy Child
Emotional Well-being

Code = MOV13

Development matters	Play and practical support
When young children have a close relationship with a caring and responsive adult, they explore from a safe place to which they can return.	Through play, young children can explore emotions beyond their normal range. Even reading about 'going on a bear hunt' can benefit a timid child.

Sample activity	Outdoor play with bikes.
Resources	A selection of bikes, cars and prams suitable for your group.
Health and safety	Ensure that bikes/cars/etc. selected for this activity are commensurate with the abilities of participating children.
Layout	A big, open space to race up and down in.
The role of the key worker	Take your small group outside and encourage them to race to the other end of the patio/play area. Resist the urge to follow them, encouraging any wanting your physical support to see how far they can get before you catch up. If your group can manage the whole length of the play area without you, stay at the other end and encourage them to race back to you. If there are one or two who are anxious to go that far without you, turn it into a chase so that the group must ride their bikes or push their prams to catch up with you.
Note	Observe sounds and facial expressions as young children express feelings of frustration or anger as they separate from a carer.
Questions to ask/ suggested interactions	• Who can ride fast enough to catch me? • Can you push your pram right to the end to catch John?
Comments	Use different settings to encourage more timid children. Work with other key workers to swap groups intermittently to encourage children to be adventurous without your participation.

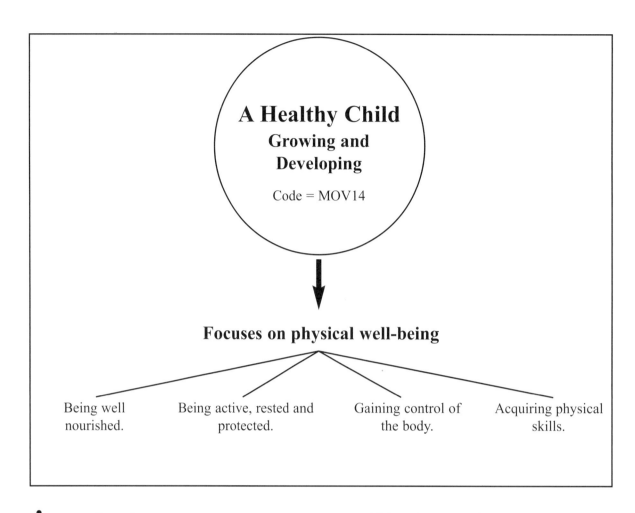

A Healthy Child
Growing and
Developing

Code = MOV14

Focuses on physical well-being

Being well
nourished.

Being active, rested and
protected.

Gaining control of
the body.

Acquiring physical
skills.

Development matters	Young children have a biological drive to use their bodies and develop their physical skills.
Look, listen, note	Note how young children develop large motor skills for walking, climbing or jumping.
Effective practice	Support, supervise and become involved as babies and children try out their developing skills.
Play and practical support	Make opportunities for young children to feed themselves using fingers, forks and spoons.

Movers, Shakers and Players

A Healthy Child
Growing and Developing

Code = MOV14

Development matters	Play and practical support
Young children have a biological drive to use their bodies and develop their physical skills.	Make opportunities for young children to feed themselves using fingers, forks and spoons.

Sample activity	Going on a bear hunt.
Resources	*We're going on a bear hunt* by M. Rosen & H. Oxenbury story book or CD.
Health and safety	There are no health and safety risks to this activity.
Layout	A big empty space and some obstacles to climb over, under or through.
The role of the key worker	If possible try not to sit reading this book, but try rather to use it for reference or, better still, join in with the story told on a tape or CD. Encourage the children to walk through 'the mud', or climb up 'the mountain' or through 'the river' using appropriate ways of walking. Remember to take them slowly in the beginning, speeding them up to test your group on the return.
Note	Note how young children develop large motor skills for walking, climbing or jumping.
Questions to ask/ suggested interactions	• Can we pretend our feet are squelching in the mud? • Phew, this mountain is high! Are we nearly there yet?
Comments	Try this using *The little prince and the great dragon chase* by Peter Kavanagh, a different story in a similar vein, but lay out the room in advance to allow searching for Teddy etc. Vary the stories to incorporate the type of physical activity you are seeking to encourage.

Movers, Shakers and Players

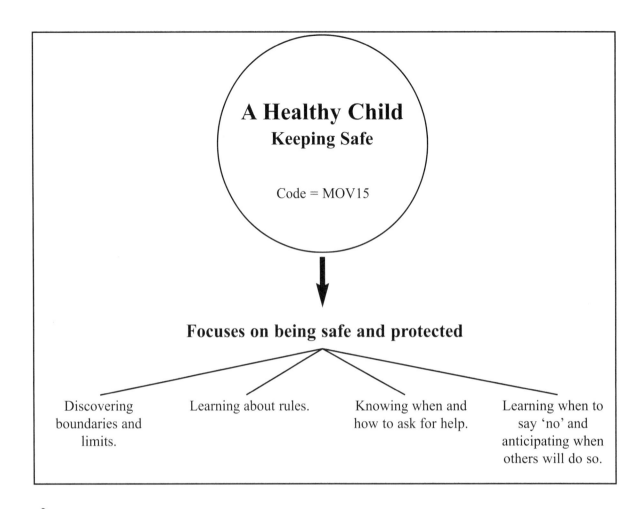

A Healthy Child
Keeping Safe

Code = MOV15

Focuses on being safe and protected

Discovering boundaries and limits.

Learning about rules.

Knowing when and how to ask for help.

Learning when to say 'no' and anticipating when others will do so.

Development matters

Given opportunities to practise what they can do in safe surroundings, young children learn some sense of danger.

Look, listen, note

Note anything that tells you about a young child's concerns and preoccupations.

Effective practice

Have agreed procedures outlining how to respond to changes in children's behaviour. Be aware of current information regarding child protection and know how to implement procedures when necessary.

Play and practical support

Have transparent boxes clearly labelled with a picture outline of the object, or the real object stuck on, so children can see where things belong and can return them safely.

Movers, Shakers and Players

A Healthy Child
Keeping Safe

Code = MOV15

Development matters	Play and practical support
Given opportunities to practise what they can do in safe surroundings, young children learn some sense of danger.	Have transparent boxes clearly labelled with a picture outline of the object, or the real object stuck on, so children can see where things belong and can return them safely.

Sample activity	Road safety in the garden.
Resources	A selection of bikes, prams etc. suitable for your age group. An improvised zebra crossing, traffic lights, lollipop and school crossing patrol outfit, police outfit.
Health and safety	There are no health and safety risks to this activity.
Layout	Set out a roadway for the bikes, a path for pedestrians and prams with the selected outfits laid out adjacent to the appropriate equipment.
The role of the key worker	With your small group encourage the children to choose which role they will play – crossing patrol, police officer, pedestrian, motorist etc. Make sure that you select one yourself. Encourage the children to play freely, but always considering the rules of the road. Change traffic lights to red and encourage cars to stop while others cross. Pedestrians at the side of the road near to a zebra crossing suggest that cars might stop ... but also might not. Talk the children through the activity, encouraging them to play safely.
Note	Note anything which tells you about a young child's concerns or preoccupations.
Questions to ask/ suggested interactions	• We have a red light. What does that mean? • Oh no! This car went through the red light. What should the police officer do?
Comments	This might be difficult where outside space is not always easily available. However, the activity can still be enjoyed indoors with children wearing cardboard box tabards to represent cars etc.

Movers, Shakers and Players

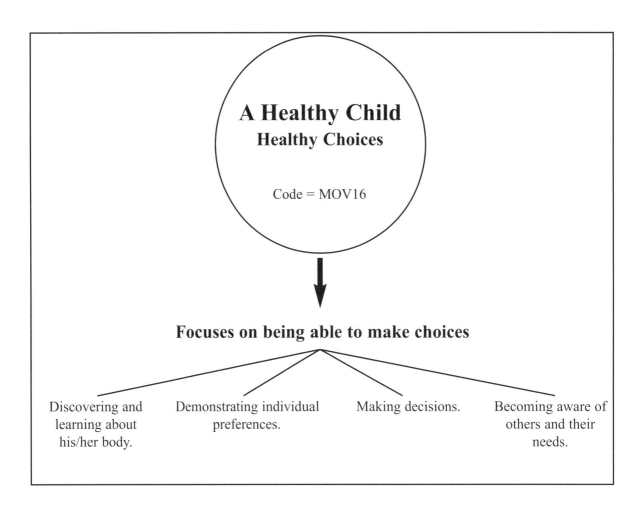

A Healthy Child
Healthy Choices

Code = MOV16

Focuses on being able to make choices

Discovering and learning about his/her body.

Demonstrating individual preferences.

Making decisions.

Becoming aware of others and their needs.

Development matters	As young children become more mobile and their boundaries widen, they make choices that can involve real risk. Adults need to ensure their safety, while not inhibiting the risk-taking.
Look, listen, note	Consider carefully how you react when a young child makes a choice you do not consider to be healthy, e.g. a child making a gun from building blocks or children always bringing sweet things to eat at snack time.
Effective practice	Create time to discuss options so that children really do have choices, e.g. whether they will drink water, juice or milk.
Play and practical support	Support children in accepting choices made by other children and adults, even when this limits their own choices.

Movers, Shakers and Players

A Healthy Child
Healthy Choices

Code = MOV16

Development matters	Play and practical support
As young children become more mobile and their boundaries widen, they make choices that can involve real risk. Adults need to ensure their safety, while not inhibiting risk-taking.	Support children in accepting choices made by other children and adults, even when this limits their own choices.

Sample activity	Safe opposites.
Resources	Make use of all of the things around you, but keep in mind unsafe issues that may have arisen in the past.
Health and safety	Care should be taken when discussing 'unsafe' opposites that they are not introducing a new and fun challenge for children to experiment with.
Layout	Sit in a circle.
The role of the key worker	Talk carefully to the children so that they can sense the importance of the subject about keeping safe. Ask the group if they know of ways that they can keep safe, but with this age do not expect much input. Start with a recent example for impact. Ask the children if they would eat a piece of toast that has fallen on the floor. Respond dramatically if any say yes: 'Ugh! No! The toast will be full of germs from the floor. Put it in the bin and get a clean piece.' Use other examples such as sitting on a table or on a chair; keeping fingers out of the way of doors etc. Take opportunities as they arise to reinforce inappropriate actions by identifying *why* they are not safe.
Note	Note how you react when a young child makes a choice that you consider to be unhealthy, e.g. a child making a gun from building blocks, or children always bringing sweet things to eat at snack time.
Questions to ask/ suggested interactions	• What might happen if we sit on that table instead of a chair? • Why don't we eat Louise's sandwich that she started?
Comments	This is an activity that can be started off in a small group discussion, but is best returned to regularly to reinforce appropriate behaviour. As the children develop, the number of examples will increase according to their increased adventurousness.

Movers, Shakers and Players

Case study

A day in the life of Amelia Smith, aged 20 months

Time	Activity	Achieved
9:25	Amelia comes into Blue Room carried by her mum. Mum passes Amelia to Claire who is sitting on the mat about to sing songs with a group of children. Amelia waves happily to her mum and settles comfortably on Claire's knee.	MOV13
9:35	This morning's planner says 'large cars and bikes outside', but it is raining so the room is cleared and other staff members get the cars and bikes out of the shed. As soon as Claire gives the group the go-ahead to play, Amelia charges right the way across the room to get to the shopping trolley before anybody else. Clearly very satisfied with her selection, she steers the trolley over to the home corner and starts putting food items in her trolley before pushing it around the room. As she passes the large black four-wheel drive the driver gets out and without hesitation Amelia lets go of her trolley and gets in. Driving her car around the room, it is really too big for her and she constantly bumps into everybody else, which she seems to find quite funny.	MOV10 MOV11
10:30	Cars and bikes tidied away, the tables are put back into place and the children will work in their key worker groups for the next session. Amelia sits right next to Luke, her key worker, and takes the magnets from his hand to stick them onto her magnetic board. She moves them around, taking magnets from other children until she is happy with her picture. Once satisfied with her picture, she moves to the other side of her table and starts on a simple jigsaw. Lee helps Amelia fit one or two pieces in and she completes the jigsaw with lots of praise from Lee. She immediately tips it out and starts again, this time completing it with lots of support but no help from Lee. After completing it a second time, she leaves her table to go and sit by another worker, Justine. Justine is playing with animal figures and her group of children, but is happy for Amelia to join in. Amelia joins in with Justine's group making animal noises.	MOV11 MOV9
11:15	Realising that Amelia's nappy needs to be changed, Justine takes her straight into the nappy change and chats away to Amelia. Amelia answers all of Justine's questions happily.	MOV16
11:30	Returning from the nappy change, the children are now seated on the mat listening to *Down by the cool of the pool*. Without hesitation Amelia climbs over several children in her way to sit by her friends in the corner. She enjoys the rest of the story, listening and repeating words as the story requires.	MOV7 MOV6
11:45	Lunchtime. Amelia sits down for dinner with her group of friends and waits as her soup is brought to her. Holding her hand out for the crusty bread, she discards her spoon and, dipping her bread into the soup, tucks in. As the bread is finished, she happily picks up her spoon and very competently empties her bowl. Luke asks her if she would like any more, she nods in response and a little more soup is ladled into her bowl. Again she finishes this easily. Shrove Tuesday means pancakes for pudding and Amelia joins in as the children cheer when the pancakes are brought into the room. With her plate in front of her, she does not even attempt to eat the pancakes but uses her spoon to scoop up the cream that accompanies them.	MOV14
12:15	After lunch Amelia goes with her group to the bathroom to have her face and hands washed. She is given a warm facecloth to wash her own face and does quite a good job. Praising her for a good job, Luke can see a spot she has missed so takes her facecloth and finishes it off for her. He then gives Amelia her toothbrush with toothpaste already on and she moves nearer to the sink and brushes her teeth using appropriate actions.	MOV14
12:30	Returning to her room, Amelia goes straight over to her floor cushion and lies down to go to sleep. Stella covers her with a blanket and without any additional support, Amelia goes straight off to sleep.	MOV14

A day in the life of Amelia Smith, aged 20 months continued

Time	Activity	Achieved
1:45	Amelia wakes on her own, lies on her cushion for a little while watching everything that goes on. After a while she gets herself up and goes to join Phil who is reading a story to a group of children.	**MOV16**
2:00	Lights on, curtains are opened and the children are offered a new selection of toys for the afternoon. Amelia chooses the sand tray and immediately begins to fill a bucket with sand using a spade. She works slowly and carefully, attempting to build a sandcastle each time the bucket is full. Sometimes it works, sometimes it doesn't but she seems to be enjoying the whole activity.	**MOV11**
2:20	After a while Amelia leaves the sand and selects the home corner. She chooses a specific doll and wraps it in a blanket and cuddles it like a baby. Holding the baby carefully, she starts to prepare dinner at the cooker. Caitlin decides to play in the home corner too. Amelia makes room for her and the two girls play happily side by side, but without conversation.	**MOV10** **MOV4**
2:45	Circle time. Lee is talking to the children about behaviour and about how good everybody has been at playing happily today. He gives out stickers to children, allowing Amelia to select which sticker she would like. As she sits down, Amelia sees the door open and her dad arrive to pick her up. She immediately runs over to him and hugs his legs. Excited at going home, she shouts 'Bye' to all her friends and they shout in return.	**MOV2** **MOV13**

Code list		Additional suggestions
A Strong Child		
MOV1	Me, Myself and I	Grouping by shoe colour; How do we travel to nursery?
MOV2	Being Acknowledged and Affirmed	Helping each other; Role playing a favourite story.
MOV3	Developing Self Assurance	Helping a younger child; What did I learn today?
MOV4	A Sense of Belonging	Bringing Mum to read a favourite story to my friends; Where do I keep my coat?
A Skilful Communicator		
MOV5	Being Together	These are my friends; Being helpful to each other.
MOV6	Finding a Voice	Taking messages to other groups; What is your name?
MOV7	Listening and Responding	Story sacks; Chinese whispers.
MOV8	Making Meaning	What shall we do next? Persona doll session.
A Competent Learner		
MOV9	Making Connections	Assault course; What can we find in our garden?
MOV10	Being Imaginative	Copycats; What did you do then? Show me . . .
MOV11	Being Creative	Fishing in jelly; When I grow up I want to be . . .
MOV12	Representing	Gloop; Write a shopping list for me.
A Healthy Child		
MOV13	Emotional Well-being	Bringing Mum to lunch; I like it when you do that!
MOV14	Growing and Developing	Discovering new tastes; Looking after our body.
MOV15	Keeping Safe	Talking about nursery rules; Can you help me?
MOV16	Healthy Choices	Potty/toilet training; I don't want to . . .

Aspect title:	
Component title:	**Code =**

Development matters	Play and practical support

Sample activity	
Resources	
Health and safety	
Layout	
The role of the key worker	
Note	
Questions to ask/ suggested interactions	• •
Comments	

Aspect title:	
Component title:	**Code =**

Development matters	Play and practical support

Sample activity	
Resources	
Health and safety	
Layout	
The role of the key worker	
Note	
Questions to ask/ suggested interactions	• •
Comments	

Movers, Shakers and Players

Completed by: **Date:**

Movers, Shakers and Players
(18–24 months)

Date of activity:	Supervised by:

Children involved:

Comments

Date of activity:	Supervised by:

Children involved:

Comments

Date of activity:	Supervised by:

Children involved:

Comments

Walkers, Talkers
and
Pretenders

(24–36 months)

Walkers, Talkers and Pretenders
(24–36 months)

Section index

Notes for this section

'Walkers, Talkers and Pretenders' – how well this heading describes the children in this group! It seems that for many in this group there is little time for rest, little patience to share, but lots and lots of walking (and running and bumping and climbing and falling), talking and pretending.

Our ratios increase in this age group to address the children's increasing independence. 'I can do it!', 'No!' or 'I want that!' are common calls from this group with clearly emerging conversational skills. Yet we are still only offering one staff member for every four children because they are still very much in need of your support. Remember that sometimes *not* offering to help is just as important as knowing when to offer help. Not asking questions, but encouraging independent exploration is very important in some activities, as is knowing exactly which question will promote the most thought from your toddler without increasing levels of frustration. Patience can be thin on the ground, while tantrums are likely to be more in evidence.

Planning activities for your group will need careful consideration to avoid one child's impatience adversely affecting the group outcomes. There will be an increasing understanding from the group, so use this to your advantage and remember to make these observations clear in developmental records.

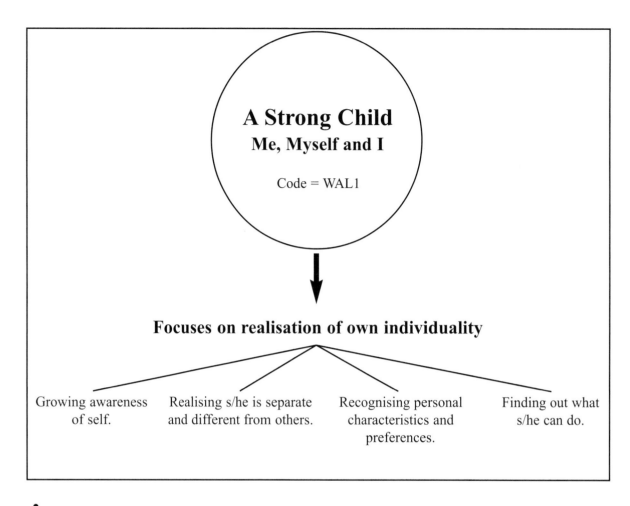

A Strong Child

Me, Myself and I

Code = WAL1

↓

Focuses on realisation of own individuality

| Growing awareness of self. | Realising s/he is separate and different from others. | Recognising personal characteristics and preferences. | Finding out what s/he can do. |

Development matters Children show their particular characteristics, preferences and interests, and demonstrate these in all they do.

Look, listen, note Note how children explore, play, socialise and make sense of their experiences.

Effective practice Practitioners who support and encourage all children enable them to gain confidence and try new things.

Play and practical support Let children make decisions about how and where to display their paintings or allow them to select which toys to play with or who to sit with.

Walkers, Talkers and Pretenders

A Strong Child
Me, Myself and I

Development matters	Play and practical support
Children show their particular characteristics, preferences and interests, and demonstrate these in all they do.	Let children make decisions about how and where to display their paintings or allow them to select which toys to play with or who to sit with.

Sample activity	Displaying a piece of free painting.
Resources	Equipment to carry out a piece of artwork. A selection of materials to back the finished result and a number of places to display it.
Health and safety	Ensure that all backing and fixing materials are appropriate to the age of children participating, providing adult support where staplers might be needed.
Layout	Lay out a selection of backing materials near to the painting corner.
The role of the key worker	Observe children painting and respond when a child seems particularly pleased with the finished article. Talk with them about their painting and ask them if they would like to put their picture up on the wall, either at nursery or at home. Ask the child if they would like you to help them back the picture once it has dried, and encourage them to select an appropriate selection of papers. Try to ensure that this is the child's work and that *you* are helping *them* to back their own picture, not worrying if it is not displayed straight unless the child wants it straight. Once backed, talk with the child about spaces available for it to be displayed, pointing out that it cannot be on top of another child's work.
Note	Note how children explore, play, socialise and make sense of their experiences.
Questions to ask/ suggested interactions	• Are there any colours in your picture that you would like to use in the backing? • Would you like to put the Blu-tack on or shall I? • Where do you think your picture would look best?
Comments	Care should be taken that pictures are not displayed on top of each other. Also bear in mind the nursery budget and only offer the children materials that you are happy using for this purpose. Expensive shiny card will look lovely as a backing, but you won't be popular with others if you use it all up in this way.

Walkers, Talkers and Pretenders

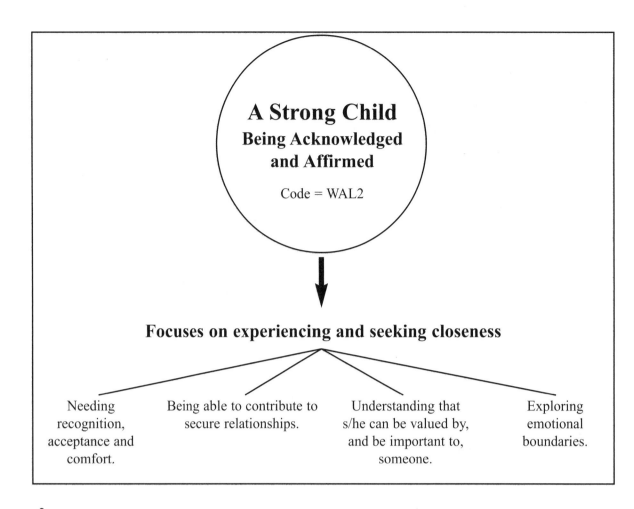

A Strong Child
Being Acknowledged
and Affirmed

Code = WAL2

Focuses on experiencing and seeking closeness

| Needing recognition, acceptance and comfort. | Being able to contribute to secure relationships. | Understanding that s/he can be valued by, and be important to, someone. | Exploring emotional boundaries. |

Development matters

Children need to feel others are positive towards them and experience realistic expectations in order to become competent, assertive and self-assured.

Look, listen, note

Note how you ensure that each child is recognised as a valuable contributor to the group, and how you celebrate cultural, religious and ethnic experiences.

Effective practice

Encourage all children to participate in making any rules and help to understand expectations and boundaries.

Play and practical support

Provide dressing up clothes and materials that help children find out what it feels like to be someone else.

Walkers, Talkers and Pretenders

A Strong Child
Being Acknowledged and Affirmed

Code = WAL2

Development matters	Play and practical support
Children need to feel others are positive towards them and experience realistic expectations in order to become competent, assertive and self-assured.	Provide dressing up clothes and materials that help children find out what it feels like to be someone else.

Sample activity	Getting to know our persona doll.
Resources	A doll (or puppet) with a clearly defined persona and life history that is familiar to the children. A familiar worker to share the discussion with the children.
Health and safety	There are no health and safety risks to this activity.
Layout	Sitting in a circle with the persona doll clearly visible to all.
The role of the key worker	Identify a recent experience that upset one of your group and use this as a basis for your story about your persona doll called Joe. Start the session by reminding the children about Joe's story and then tell the group that Joe was upset the other day when somebody snatched his toy and wouldn't give it him back. Encourage the children to empathise and tell you how they would feel if somebody did that to them. Ask the children what they might do if somebody did that to them and offer a suggestion from Joe that you feel might be the best answer. Also ask the children to consider what they might do if they saw somebody being unkind to somebody else and again respond with Joe's thoughts. Remember to close the session on a positive with lots of hugs for Joe and each other.
Note	Note how you ensure that each child is recognised as a valuable contributor to the group and how you celebrate cultural, religious and ethnic experiences.
Questions to ask/ suggested interactions	• Why do you think Joe felt upset? • What could you do to help him? • Why do you think Asham took Joe's toy?
Comments	Remember to use your persona doll for fun and positive experiences otherwise the children might begin to associate his visits with a lecture. If you do not have an official persona doll, there is no problem with you identifying another doll to take on this role. Try to ensure that its life history is agreed with all workers beforehand as any conflicts in stories from one worker to another *will* be picked up by the children.

Walkers, Talkers and Pretenders

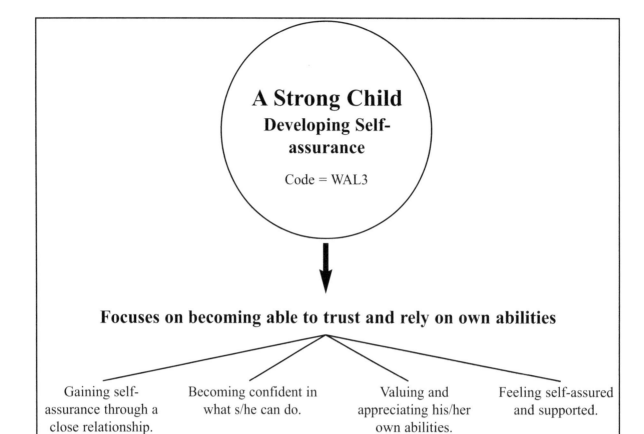

A Strong Child
Developing Self-assurance

Code = WAL3

Focuses on becoming able to trust and rely on own abilities

Gaining self-assurance through a close relationship.

Becoming confident in what s/he can do.

Valuing and appreciating his/her own abilities.

Feeling self-assured and supported.

Development matters

To appreciate what they can do independently children need relationships, through which they develop self-confidence, a belief in themselves and healthy self-esteem.

Look, listen, note

Note how children express their own confidence and sense of self-assurance by showing they value what they and others do.

Effective practice

Clear and consistent expectations and trust in children's abilities will help to increase their self-confidence and show you value and appreciate their efforts.

Play and practical support

Talk to children about an activity and discuss with them what resources they need and where they might find them. Then encourage them to get things for themselves, so developing their sense of self-assurance.

Walkers, Talkers and Pretenders

A Strong Child
Developing Self-assurance

Code = WAL3

Development matters	Play and practical support
To appreciate what they can do independently children need relationships, through which they develop self-confidence, a belief in themselves and healthy self-esteem.	Talk to children about an activity and discuss with them what resources they need and where they might find them. Then encourage them to get things for themselves, so developing their sense of self-assurance.

Sample activity	Can I help you?
Resources	Coats and hats etc. for outdoors play. A group of co-operative and helpful children!
Health and safety	There are no health and safety risks to this activity, but care should be taken to ensure that help offered is carefully administered.
Layout	Take a small group of children to collect the coats and hats that they might need for playing outside and bring them into the room so that there is room enough to move about fairly freely.
The role of the key worker	Pair children up with each other and ask if they can help each other get ready for playing outdoors. At the beginning show children how to hold their friend's coat so that it is easier to put on, but in later sessions try to leave them to it. Encourage the children to talk in their pairs about what is helpful, but also be trusting that their friends can help. Praise children who work well co-operatively together even if the end result needs input from you. Praise the children as a group for being clever and helpful to each other.
Note	Note how children express their own confidence and self-assurance by showing they value what they and others do.
Questions to ask/ suggested interactions	• Which arm do you think Alex should put in her coat first? • Can you hold the coat higher so that James can reach it easier?
Comments	Being helpful to somebody is a great way of gaining self-assurance, but be aware that younger or less able children might feel very frustrated if they cannot be helpful. Direct these pairs to help in different ways, such as helping to find the coat, or putting on a hat rather than a coat.

Walkers, Talkers and Pretenders

A Strong Child

A Sense of Belonging

Code = WAL4

Focuses on acquiring social confidence and competence

| Being able to snuggle in. | Enjoying being with familiar and trusted others. | Valuing individuality and contributions of self and others. | Having a role and identity within a group. |

Development matters

The development of a strong sense of identity both individually and within a group helps children feel they belong.

Look, listen, note

Observe the strategies children use to join in or avoid a group during play.

Effective practice

Encourage all children to participate in and contribute in a group, being mindful that some will find this more difficult than others.

Play and practical support

Provide a soft toy for children to take home in turn. It could have an overnight bag with a note to parents encouraging them, with their child, to care for it and return it safely.

Walkers, Talkers and Pretenders

A Strong Child

A Sense of Belonging

Development matters	Play and practical support
The development of a strong sense of identity both individually and within a group helps children to feel they belong.	Provide a soft toy for children to take home in turn. It could have an overnight bag with a note to parents encouraging them, with their child, to care for it and return it safely.

Sample activity	Roll call.
Resources	Flash cards with each child's photograph and first name on it.
Health and safety	There are no health and safety risks to this activity.
Layout	Sit in a circle with your key group.
The role of the key worker	Sitting the children together, start with the first name on the top and ask 'Who is this?' When the children respond, ask 'Is Max here?' If he is, welcome him to the session and encourage his friends to shake his hand or give him a hug. If he isn't in, ask the children if they can think what he might be doing instead, letting them know if he is having a day off with Gran, or is ill so that they can sympathise. Go through the whole group, welcoming everybody including other key workers.
Note	Observe the strategies children use to join in or avoid a group during play.
Questions to ask/ suggested interactions	• Max is not here, what do you think he might be doing? • Jim wasn't very well yesterday, do you think he will feel better soon? • Rachel had a day off yesterday. Can you tell us about your day?
Comments	Remember to ask children about their day if they weren't in, or if they feel better after being ill. Remember to prepare new cards for children joining the group immediately so that they can feel a part of the group straightaway.

Walkers, Talkers and Pretenders

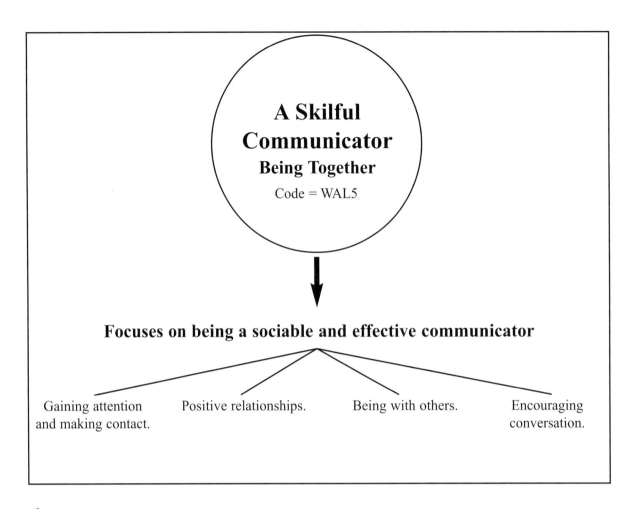

A Skilful
Communicator
Being Together
Code = WAL5

Focuses on being a sociable and effective communicator

Gaining attention
and making contact.

Positive relationships.

Being with others.

Encouraging
conversation.

Development matters	Children learn social skills and enjoy being with and talking to adults and other children.
Look, listen, note	Observe the ways in which young children make friends and note the attachments they make with adults and children, e.g. giving an object and taking it back.
Effective practice	Create areas in which to sit and chat with friends, e.g. a space under stairs with bright cushions, an outdoor den.
Play and practical support	Provide opportunities for all children to become part of a group, encouraging conversation.

Walkers, Talkers and Pretenders

A Skilful Communicator

Being Together

Development matters	Play and practical support
Children learn social skills and enjoy being with and talking to adults and other children.	Provide opportunities for all children to become part of a group, encouraging conversation.

Sample activity	Daily news session.
Resources	Nothing required, but paper and writing/drawing implements are an optional extra.
Health and safety	Ensure that writing implements are appropriate to this age group.
Layout	Select a comfortable area to sit and chat, providing sofas or cushions to make your group feel comfortable.
The role of the key worker	Start the ball rolling by telling the group of something that you did recently that they might be interested in. Ask them if they might like to do that, or have done it before. Move on to a child in your group and ask what they did the day before or at the weekend. Encourage the rest of the group to listen carefully to what their friend is telling them. Try not to worry about taking turns if a child has news that relates to the conversation in hand, encouraging patience while listening to the news of others. Give all of the group an opportunity to tell their news, but don't press a child who cannot think of anything to say.
Note	Observe the ways in which young children make friends and note the attachments they make with adults and children, e.g. giving an object and taking it back.
Questions to ask/ suggested interactions	• Hannah, were you about to tell us that you went to McDonald's at the weekend too? • Ava, did you forget that you went to visit your auntie in Wales? • Can we all listen to Leyleh's news and then we can chat about your news?
Comments	Take care to ensure that all of the children in your group do participate over a period of time, but it is not necessary that they do so every time. Talk with parents to find out news for a child who regularly finds it difficult to contribute and ask them about that specific item.

Walkers, Talkers and Pretenders

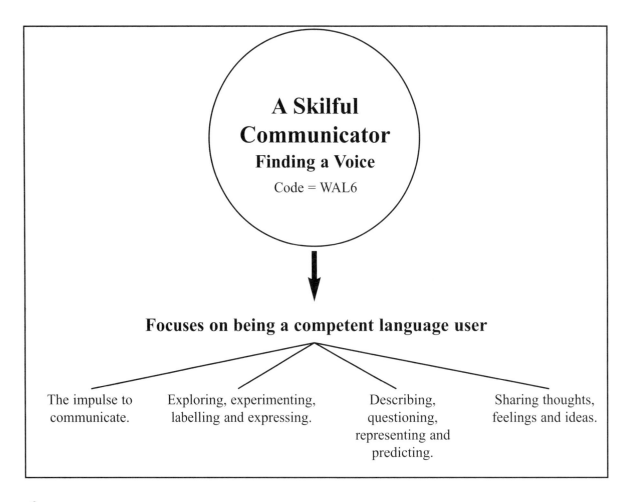

Development matters

Children use language as a powerful means of widening contacts, sharing feelings, experiences and thoughts.

Look, listen, note

Note what children say as they begin to combine words, ask questions, describe and predict.

Effective practice

Opportunities for children to talk with other children, visitors and other adults about what they see, hear, think and feel.

Play and practical support

Role play and dressing up, visits to parks, shops or libraries encourage children to take on roles, meet others, and express feelings and thoughts.

Walkers, Talkers and Pretenders

A Skilful Communicator
Finding a Voice

Development matters	Play and practical support
Children use language as a powerful means of widening contacts, sharing feelings, experiences and thoughts.	Role play and dressing up, visits to parks, shops or libraries encourage children to take on roles, meet others, and express feelings and thoughts.

Sample activity	Role play: going to a restaurant.
Resources	Dressing up clothes to provide waiters/waitresses, chefs, customers on a posh night out etc. A dinner service/tea set/kitchen equipment and menu to choose from.
Health and safety	Ensure that all role play implements are appropriate to this age group.
Layout	Set out the area for one or two tables of diners depending on the size of your group, a kitchen to cook in etc.
The role of the key worker	Talk to the children about their experiences in restaurants and agree who will be staff and who will be customers. Encourage the children to select their favourite dishes to eat while the waiter writes down their selection and takes it into the kitchen for the chef to prepare. Talk about things we might do at a restaurant and encourage the children to chat about their own experiences or thoughts.
Note	Note what children say as they begin to combine words, ask questions, describe and predict.
Questions to ask/ suggested interactions	• Who has been to a restaurant with waiters and waitresses? • What did they do? • How is a table set at a restaurant?
Comments	Vary the role play to encourage different topics of conversation, but also to coincide with experiences of the children in your group – hospital, vets, hairdressers etc.

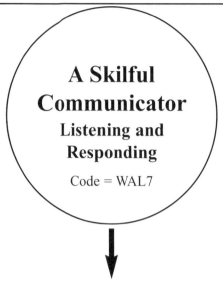

A Skilful Communicator
Listening and Responding

Code = WAL7

Focuses on listening and responding appropriately to the language of others

| Listening and paying attention to what others say. | Making playful and serious responses. | Enjoying and sharing stories, songs, rhymes and games. | Learning about words and meanings. |

Development matters

Children learn new words very rapidly and are able to use them in talking about matters which interest them.

Look, listen, note

Note how children begin to use words in context, e.g. in questioning, imitating with understanding, playing, negotiating.

Effective practice

Extend the range of stories, songs, games and rhymes from their own and other cultures and languages.

Play and practical support

Use familiar photographs to introduce new words and encourage responses from children.

Walkers, Talkers and Pretenders

A Skilful Communicator
Listening and Responding

Development matters	Play and practical support
Children learn new words very rapidly and are able to use them in talking about matters which interest them.	Use familiar photographs to introduce new words and encourage responses from children.

Sample activity	Who can leap like a little lamb?
Resources	None really required, but pictures of the animals you might be using may come in handy.
Health and safety	There are no health and safety risks to this activity.
Layout	A large, empty space with comfortable flooring.
The role of the key worker	Start with some phrases that the children are familiar with and ask them to run like a rabbit or moo like a cow. Move in to new descriptives, demonstrating how to do it if the children look puzzled. Use phrases such as: Slither like a snake, leap like a lamb or pounce like a tiger.
Note	Note how children begin to use words in context, e.g. in questioning, imitating with understanding, playing, negotiating.
Questions to ask/ suggested interactions	• Who knows what a kangaroo does? • Kangaroos jump, but what else can we call that? • Can we remember the words we have learnt today?
Comments	Try to make yourself lists of groups of words to use in future sessions. Try different types of housing, transport, painting techniques etc.

Walkers, Talkers and Pretenders

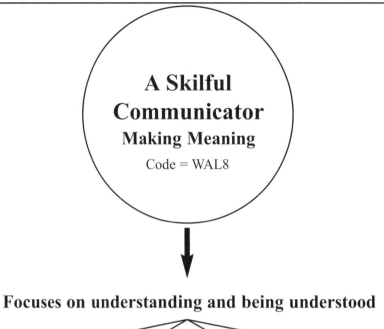

A Skilful Communicator
Making Meaning
Code = WAL8

Focuses on understanding and being understood

Communicating meaning.

Influencing others.

Negotiating and making choices.

Understanding each other.

Development matters

As vocabulary increases, children make sense of the world through bargaining, negotiating, questioning, describing and labelling.

Look, listen, note

From what children do and say, note how they show what they understand, e.g. actions, questions, new words.

Effective practice

Talk to children about choices, reasons for doing things in a certain way and explain why sometimes you say 'no'.

Play and practical support

Provide play situations in which children can take on different roles and adults can help them to communicate, e.g. home, shop, hospital play.

Walkers, Talkers and Pretenders

A Skilful Communicator
Making Meaning

Code = WAL8

Development matters	Play and practical support
As vocabulary increases, children make sense of the world through bargaining, negotiating, questioning, describing and labelling.	Provide play situations in which children can take on different roles and adults can help them to communicate, e.g. home, shop, hospital play.

Sample activity	Making a deal.
Resources	Whatever it is that the children are hoping to do as well as what you are planning to do.
Health and safety	There are no health and safety risks to this activity.
Layout	Your usual activity space.
The role of the key worker	This is an opportunity to seize whenever the children are a little reluctant to do whatever you have planned. Sitting calmly in your group, explain to the children that it is not time for your group to play with the hamster or whatever it is. Tell them that if they help you tidy up really carefully you might be able to find time with the hamster when Group 2 have finished. For some children this will be immediately acceptable, but for others they may need regular reminders while tidying up to get the task finished.
Note	From what children do and say, note how they show what they understand, e.g. actions, questions, new words.
Questions to ask/ suggested interactions	• Do you think we can make a deal? • If I do that for you, will you do that for me? • If you let James play with that toy for five more minutes you can have it next. Is that okay?
Comments	Be careful not to promise anything that you cannot deliver. Also, take care not to make your bargaining points too far in the future so that the children are likely to forget about them. Try other simpler bargaining techniques in between, such as 'I'll draw you this picture if you help me sharpen these pencils.'

Walkers, Talkers and Pretenders

151

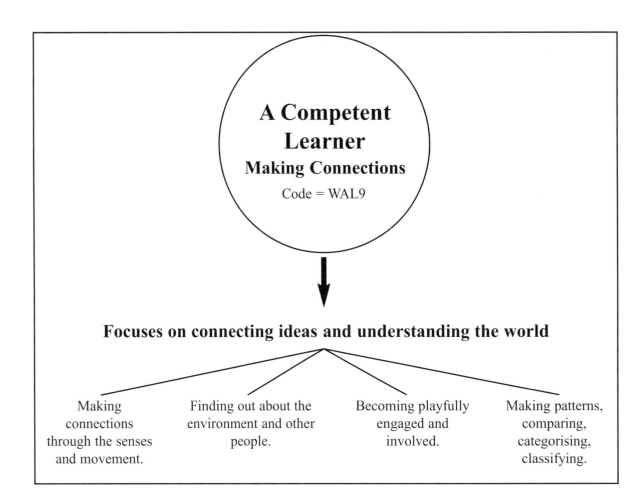

A Competent
Learner
Making Connections
Code = WAL9

Focuses on connecting ideas and understanding the world

| Making connections through the senses and movement. | Finding out about the environment and other people. | Becoming playfully engaged and involved. | Making patterns, comparing, categorising, classifying. |

Development matters

Children begin to connect objects and ideas: a *pair* of socks, a *big* teddy, armbands for swimming.

Look, listen, note

Note those children who distinguish between big and small blocks, or know when tidying up, that different kinds of toys go in different containers.

Effective practice

Use everyday experiences to help children count and focus on patterns and shapes.

Play and practical support

Thoroughly investigate environments with children, e.g. when outside consider how to shift leaves off a path, enlarge a puddle, collect water dripping from a tap.

Walkers, Talkers and Pretenders

A Competent Learner
Making Connections

Code = WAL9

Development matters	Play and practical support
Children begin to connect objects and ideas: a *pair* of socks, a *big* teddy, armbands for swimming.	Thoroughly investigate environments with children, e.g. when outside consider how to shift leaves off a path, enlarge a puddle, or collect water from a dripping tap.

Sample activity	Matching and making sets.
Resources	Either a selection of different items that are half of a pair or part of a set or photographs to represent such items.
Health and safety	Sensible selection of items for inclusion should mean that there are no health and safety risks in this activity.
Layout	A table with chairs around. A pile of your gathered items in the middle.
The role of the key worker	Introduce your session to the children by talking about things that are pairs or sets that the children are familiar with. Start with the most obvious and find one of two socks (for example) from the pile, asking the children if they can find the other. Move on to other simple pairs before changing slightly and going for a set like toothbrush and toothpaste, or umbrella and raincoat etc.
Note	Note those children who distinguish between big and small blocks, or know when tidying up, that different kinds of toys go in different containers.
Questions to ask/ suggested interactions	• What might we use this umbrella for? • So which of these things might we pair it with? • Can we pair this umbrella with anything else?
Comments	Remember that the children might see pairs or sets that you hadn't predicted, but these are not wrong. Using the examples above, the children might pair the wellies with the raincoat, but this, of course, is also correct.

Walkers, Talkers and Pretenders

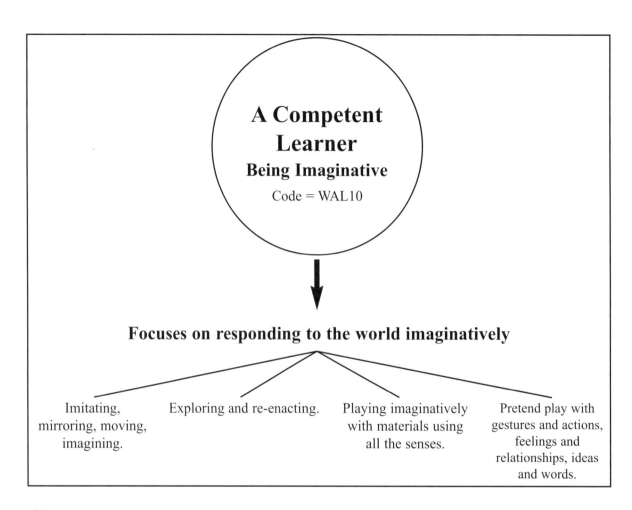

A Competent Learner
Being Imaginative
Code = WAL10

Focuses on responding to the world imaginatively

Imitating, mirroring, moving, imagining.

Exploring and re-enacting.

Playing imaginatively with materials using all the senses.

Pretend play with gestures and actions, feelings and relationships, ideas and words.

Development matters	Children engage in concentrated imaginative play in which they extend their language and try out ideas, feelings, relationships and movements.
Look, listen, note	Listen to the words children use in their imaginative play and note the learning they are displaying.
Effective practice	Adults who play and talk with children and who encourage them to express themselves imaginatively.
Play and practical support	Create spaces and opportunities for quiet and noisy play, providing opportunities for adults and children to act as playmates, observers, initiators.

Walkers, Talkers and Pretenders

A Competent Learner
Being Imaginative
Code = WAL10

Development matters	Play and practical support
Children engage in concentrated imaginative play in which they extend their language and try out ideas, feelings, relationships and movements.	Create spaces and opportunities for quiet and noisy play, providing opportunities for adults and children to act as playmates, observers and initiators.

Sample activity	Fabric play.
Resources	A wide selection of different fabrics in different lengths and sizes. Remember to include different textures such as PVC, netting, voile and sari or curtain materials. Add to this a selection of shoes, hats, bags etc.
Health and safety	Close supervision is necessary to ensure there is no risk of strangulation from some of the fabrics such as scarves.
Layout	Start this session by draping the different selections over a chair and spreading the chairs around the space you have available.
The role of the key worker	There should be little instruction required before the children are creatively involved in this session. Watch as they wrap themselves in different fabrics and match them with shoes to create a complete image. Make suggestions to those children who seem a little lost for a starting point, such as: 'If we choose this shiny material and those silver wellies, we could pretend to be an astronaut.' Provide help to those struggling with extra long pieces of fabric and, of course, watch to make sure that fabrics do not become tightly wrapped around necks.
Note	Listen to the words children use in their imaginative play and note the learning they are displaying.
Questions to ask/ suggested interactions	• What do you think we can do with this rubbery piece of material? • Why not try teaming it up with these wellies and this sou'wester and becoming a fisherman?
Comments	Providing as many different types of hats, bags, shoes, necklaces and other props will extend or alter this activity significantly. Try leaving some of the pieces in the dressing up box, but keeping some of them aside to make this session different from just dressing up.

Walkers, Talkers and Pretenders

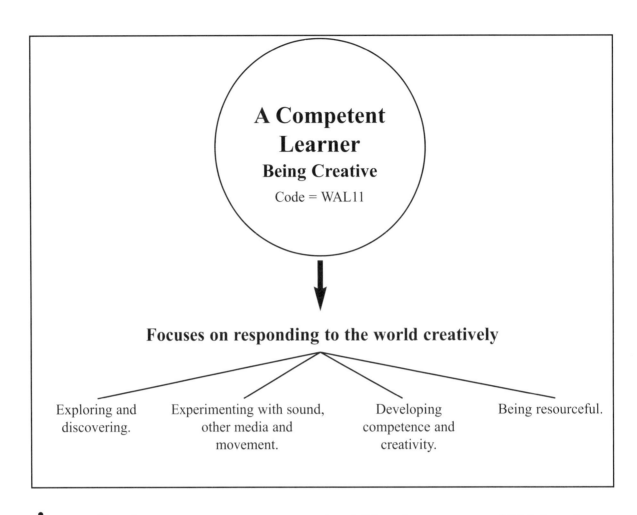

A Competent Learner
Being Creative
Code = WAL11

Focuses on responding to the world creatively

Exploring and discovering.

Experimenting with sound, other media and movement.

Developing competence and creativity.

Being resourceful.

Development matters

As children become more skilful in using language and other forms of communication such as dance, music, 2D and 3D art, they talk about, and share in other ways, the things they paint, draw and play with.

Look, listen, note

Watch how children with a specific sensory impairment use other senses in order to enjoy experiences.

Effective practice

Provide children with a range of materials to help them to represent their unique and individual perception of the world, unrestricted by adult ideas, e.g. rabbits need not have whiskers made of drinking straws.

Play and practical support

A collection of everyday objects such as wooden pegs, spoons, pans, corks, cones and boxes can be explored alone or shared with adults or other children.

Walkers, Talkers and Pretenders

A Competent Learner
Being Creative

Development matters	Play and practical support
As children become more skilful in using language and other forms of communication such as dance, music, 2D and 3D art, they talk about, and share in other ways, the things they paint, draw and play with.	A collection of everyday objects such as wooden pegs, spoons, pans, corks, cones and boxes can be explored alone or shared with adults or other children.

Sample activity	Junk modelling.
Resources	A large selection of different objects. Glue, sticky tape, staples (with adult supervision) and other fixings. Paint in different forms. Aprons.
Health and safety	Ensure that objects are not in danger of transmitting nut or other food allergies. Other food items must be thoroughly washed before use. Use of staples and sticky tape should be supervised.
Layout	Try to collect the goods in boxes that the children can root around in, ensuring that small things do not get lost at the bottom. Set the boxes out in one area, with the fixings in another and paint in another area.
The role of the key worker	If the children are unfamiliar with this type of activity, start with a strange or interesting looking piece and ask one of your group: 'What can we make with this?' or 'What does this look like?' to get the ball rolling. Try not to direct the building, but offer help and support with fixings or if a child appears to be frustrated because paint won't stick to the washing-up bottle. Try to ensure that there is a long time available for this session to allow children plenty of time to finish their piece. Put it somewhere safe to dry and display it well once completed.
Note	Watch how children with a specific sensory impairment use other senses in order to enjoy experiences.
Questions to ask/ suggested interactions	• What does this look like? • What can we turn this into? • Would you like me to help you with that?
Comments	Be aware of the frustrations of junk modelling before starting this session, and be prepared. PVA is great, but won't stick plastic to plastic easily so be prepared to offer alternatives. Take care not to use food packaging that may have contained nuts or nut derivatives.

Walkers, Talkers and Pretenders

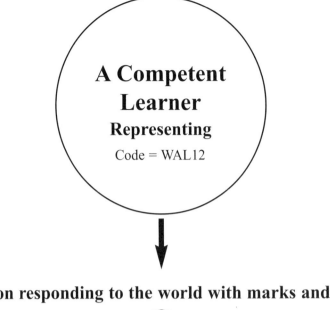

A Competent Learner

Representing

Code = WAL12

Focuses on responding to the world with marks and symbols

| Exploring, experimenting and playing. | Discovering that one thing can stand for another. | Creating and experimenting with one's own symbols and marks. | Recognising that others may use marks differently. |

Development matters — Children begin to recognise some marks and realise these mean something to others.

Look, listen, note — Note all the marks that children make and how they 'tell' you what their 'products' mean.

Effective practice — Provide materials that reflect a cultural spread so that children see symbols and marks with which they are familiar, e.g. Arabic script on bags from the local shop, Chinese writing on a poster, or introduce a 'feely' book for a child who is blind.

Play and practical support — Focus on meaningful print such as the child's name, favourite cereal or book, in order to discuss similarities and differences between symbols.

Walkers, Talkers and Pretenders

A Competent Learner
Representing

Development matters	Play and practical support
Children begin to recognise some marks and realise these mean something to others.	Focus on meaningful print such as the child's name, favourite cereal or book, in order to discuss similarities and differences between symbols.

Sample activity	Sign lotto.
Resources	Gather together a selection of signs that are familiar to the children from their environment and copy them onto lotto cards. Choose stop and go signs, crossing patrol lollipops, no entry, familiar shop logos etc.
Health and safety	There are no health and safety risks to this activity.
Layout	Select a table for your session with enough chairs around the side for your group.
The role of the key worker	Sit with your group around the table each with a lotto card. Start with the first symbol and ask: 'Matthew, can you tell me what this symbol means?' If Matthew can tell you, praise him and then ask who has this symbol on their card. If Matthew can't tell you, encourage the others to help him. Continue in this way until all of your symbols are gone, encouraging all of the children to tell you what they mean and help others.
Note	Note all the marks children make and how they 'tell' you what their 'products' mean.
Questions to ask/ suggested interactions	• Who can help Matthew remember what this symbol means? • Does anybody have a matching symbol on their card? • Where might we see this symbol in nursery?
Comments	An alternative way to play with these symbols is to have the children show you what the symbol means to them and encourage them to mime eating for the big yellow 'M' symbol etc.

Walkers, Talkers and Pretenders

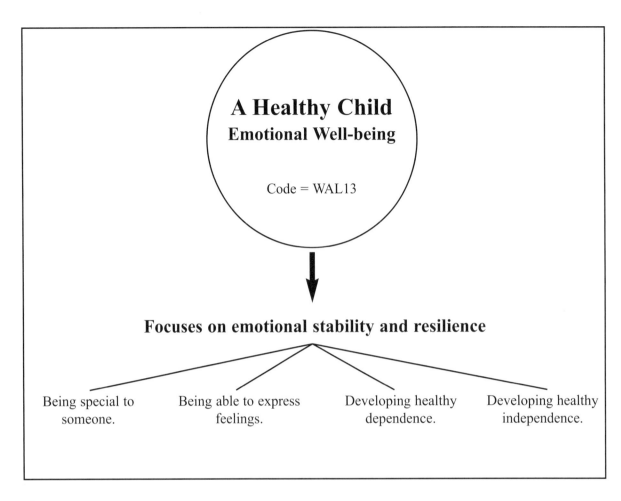

A Healthy Child
Emotional Well-being

Code = WAL13

Focuses on emotional stability and resilience

Being special to someone.

Being able to express feelings.

Developing healthy dependence.

Developing healthy independence.

Development matters	As children learn to do things for themselves they gain confidence, knowing that the adult is close by, ready to support and help if needed.
Look, listen, note	Note examples of healthy independence, e.g. a child playing happily at building, or looking through a window.
Effective practice	Recognition that children need a predictable environment in which to feel safe and that their independence may be affected temporarily by changes of staff or by moving to another room.
Play and practical support	Provide stories, pictures and puppets, which allow children to experience and talk about feelings.

Walkers, Talkers and Pretenders

A Healthy Child
Emotional Well-being

Development matters	Play and practical support
As children learn to do things for themselves they gain confidence, knowing that the adult is close by, ready to support and help if needed.	Provide stories, pictures and puppets, which allow children to experience and talk about feelings.

Sample activity	Going to the toilet.
Resources	The nursery bathroom with appropriate toileting supplies.
Health and safety	All usual health and safety risk assessments related to toileting should be undertaken.
Layout	Nothing specific required.
The role of the key worker	When a child has mastered the use of the toilet and is comfortable taking himself to the toilet, it can sometimes be a bit frustrating when clothing is not 'very helpful' and gets in the way. Accompany the child to the toilet as usual, but allow them to manage on their own as best they can. Watch closely for potential areas of frustration such as buckles or buttons, or if they come rushing in from playing outside and still have their coat on. Ask: 'Would you like me to help?' without assuming that the answer will be 'yes', and wait for a response before helping. Do only as much as is necessary to help the child continue, perhaps stopping when the troublesome button is undone. Praise the child for doing so much on their own and for remembering to ask for help in time.
Note	Note examples of healthy independence, e.g. a child playing happily with building blocks or looking through a window.
Questions to ask/ suggested interactions	• Would you like me to help you with that button? • Can you manage on your own? • Is that all you need me to do?
Comments	Make sure that your support does not undermine the child's ability and does not impinge on the child's self-esteem.

Walkers, Talkers and Pretenders

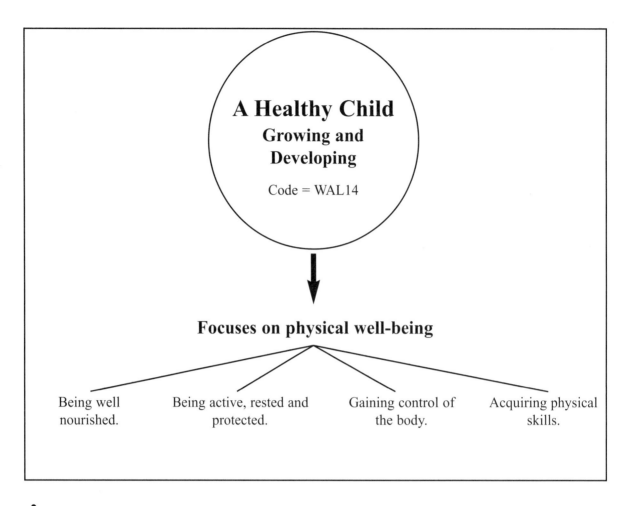

A Healthy Child
Growing and
Developing

Code = WAL14

Focuses on physical well-being

Being well nourished.

Being active, rested and protected.

Gaining control of the body.

Acquiring physical skills.

Development matters	Children only gradually gain control of their whole bodies.
Look, listen, note	Look for ways in which children begin to develop fine motor skills, e.g. the way they use their fingers in trying to do up buttons on a coat, pull up a zip, pour a drink, use a watering can.
Effective practice	Support children's growing independence as they strive to gain control of their bladders and bowels by offering flexible routines and by encouraging and valuing effort.
Play and practical support	Offer choices for children such as potties, small toilets, trainer seats, steps, and recognise and support their fascination with bodily functions.

Walkers, Talkers and Pretenders

A Healthy Child
Growing and Developing

Code = WAL14

Development matters	Play and practical support
Children only gradually gain control of their whole bodies.	Offer choices for children in terms of potties, small toilets, trainer seats, steps, and recognise and support their fascination with bodily functions.

Sample activity	Getting ourselves dressed.
Resources	Hats, coats, wellies etc. belonging to each of the group.
Health and safety	There are no health and safety risks to this activity.
Layout	Collect coats etc. from the pegs and take them into a room with plenty of space.
The role of the key worker	Try to encourage the children to do as much for themselves as possible without leaving them to it completely. Try showing them with your own coat that one arm goes in first while you reach around the back to put your other arm in the sleeve behind you. This is a difficult thing to get used to, so be patient. Once the coat is on, see if the children can do any or all of the fastenings on their coats, offering guidance to get children started or secure their fastening. Use exaggerated finger/hand movements to demonstrate, providing lots of support for those who don't want help.
Note	Look for ways in which children begin to develop fine motor skills, e.g. the way they use their fingers in trying to do up buttons on a coat, pull up a zip, pour a drink or use a watering can.
Questions to ask/ suggested interactions	• Can you reach your arm down and backwards to reach that sleeve? • Shall I hold the coat still so that you can find the opening to that sleeve? • Shall I do the first button and you can try the second?
Comments	How much support a child needs or wants may vary considerably from day to day depending on the coat and the clothes they are wearing. Support attempts to fasten buttons even if they are done up in the wrong order, not necessarily redoing them in the right way . . . after all, does it matter that they are done up incorrectly? Probably not. Praise the child for managing their buttons so well.

Walkers, Talkers and Pretenders

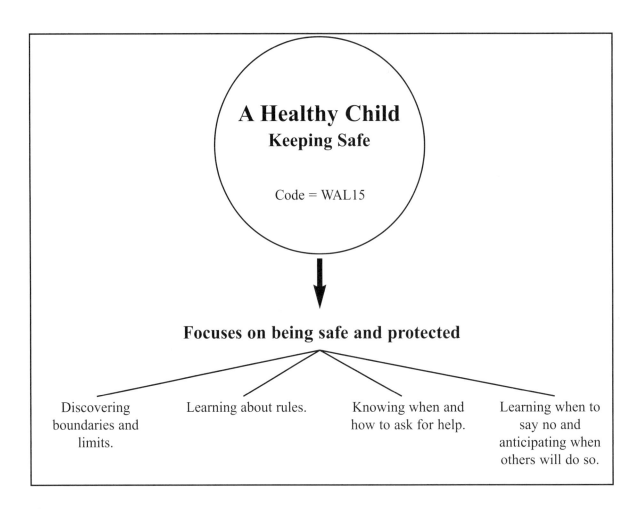

A Healthy Child
Keeping Safe

Code = WAL15

Focuses on being safe and protected

Discovering boundaries and limits.

Learning about rules.

Knowing when and how to ask for help.

Learning when to say no and anticipating when others will do so.

Development matters

Children's need for affection, attention and being special in some way makes them particularly vulnerable in relation to keeping safe.

Look, listen, note

Note the way in which children respond to different people. Always listen to what they tell adults about their experiences.

Effective practice

Maintain regular, informal communication with parents which develops strong partnerships between all those involved in keeping children safe.

Play and practical support

Talk with parents about a consistent approach when responding to challenging behaviour such as scratching and biting.

Walkers, Talkers and Pretenders

A Healthy Child
Keeping Safe

Development matters	Play and practical support
Children's need for affection, attention and being special in some way makes them particularly vulnerable in relation to keeping safe.	Talk with parents about a consistent approach when responding to challenging behaviour such as scratching and biting.

Sample activity	Learning about 'No!'
Resources	A list of scenarios that you might discuss, particularly issues that have arisen in your group recently.
Health and safety	There are no health and safety risks to this activity.
Layout	Circle time.
The role of the key worker	Sitting with your group talk about what 'no' means. Give an example that is common to your group, such as: 'Are we ready to go in yet?' while playing outside. Discuss what the 'no' response means in this situation. Change to another common situation, where a child might want a toy that you have. They ask for the toy and you say 'no'. What does this mean? So what might you feel like if they snatch the toy from you? Ask the children why the child may have taken it even though the answer was 'no'. Give the children options about what to do if this happens. Ask them if it is okay to hit out or bite or shout, or is it better to ask for help from an adult? Change the scenario and talk about another situation until you feel that the children are getting the message ... but be careful not to bore them!
Note	Note the way in which children respond to different people. Always listen to what they tell adults about their experiences.
Questions to ask/ suggested interactions	• Why do you think Anita might say 'no' if you want more dinner? • What can you do if somebody has taken your toy? • What do you do if somebody keeps saying no, you can't play with them?
Comments	Try to keep a list of occasions where 'no' has been used to little effect. Use this as an example in future sessions, possibly reinforcing this with a persona doll session.

Walkers, Talkers and Pretenders

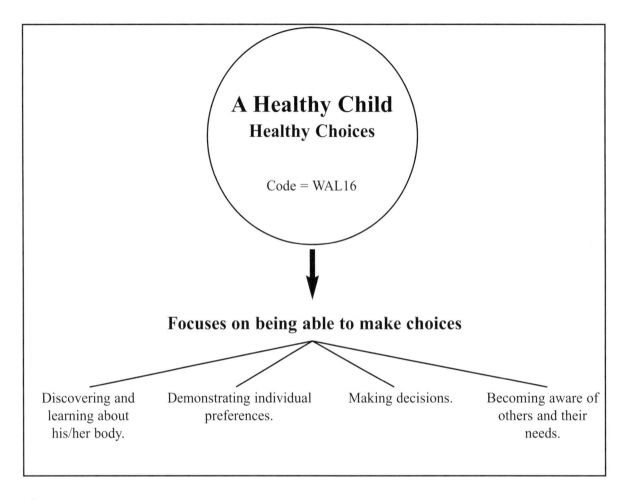

A Healthy Child
Healthy Choices

Code = WAL16

Focuses on being able to make choices

Discovering and learning about his/her body.

Demonstrating individual preferences.

Making decisions.

Becoming aware of others and their needs.

Development matters	Children become more aware that choices have consequences.
Look, listen, note	Watch the way children choose not to do things, as well as choose to do them. Note any patterns in what children consistently choose to do.
Effective practice	Engage with parents in discussions about the choices offered within the setting.
Play and practical support	Provide non-specific play materials such as boxes and blankets so that play can move in different directions.

Walkers, Talkers and Pretenders

A Healthy Child
Healthy Choices

Code = WAL16

Development matters	Play and practical support
Children become more aware that choices have consequences.	Provide non-specific play materials such as boxes and blankets so that play can move in different directions.

Sample activity	What happens if . . . ?
Resources	Nothing in particular is necessary.
Health and safety	There are no health and safety risks to this activity.
Layout	Circle time.
The role of the key worker	Talk with your group about what it means to make choices. By this age they should be familiar with choices such as which table to play on, or who to sit by, but introducing the notion that choices might have consequences is often a difficult concept to grasp. Start with obvious questions, such as: 'What happens if we play out in the rain with no coat on?' and encourage the children to identify the consequences and why a particular choice might not be good/sensible etc. Include silly options, like what happens if I put ketchup on my cornflakes, and identify that although it won't taste very nice, it isn't really important. Move on to scenarios that require a little more common sense, such as: 'What happens if I jump up and down standing on my chair?' Hopefully the children will identify that they might fall off, they might hurt themselves or they might hurt others and agree that it would be sensible to choose not to do this.
Note	Watch the way children choose not to do things, as well as choose to do them. Note any patterns in what children consistently choose to do.
Questions to ask/ suggested interactions	• What happens if I eat the sand out of the sand tray? • Does it matter if I put my shoes on the wrong feet? • What happens if I don't come when somebody calls me?
Comments	Vary your scenarios according to the children joining in, trying wherever possible to use situations that could be feasible in nursery.

Walkers, Talkers and Pretenders

Case study

A day in the life of Max Miller, aged 32 months

Time	Activity	Achieved
08:00	Max is first to arrive at nursery this morning and rushes straight in to Red Room to see who is in. He stops short in his tracks at the sight of no other children and seems confused about what to do next. Catherine can see his indecision and asks him what he'd like to do. Mum pops her head into the room to say goodbye to Max and he runs over to give her a hug, then immediately runs over to Catherine and puts himself on her knee. They sit and play with the dinosaurs on the table for quite some time, until other children arrive for him to run around with.	WAL4
08:30	It is time for Max's larger group to move through to their own location and Max joins Justine shouting 'Blue Room' to gather his friends together. Without any instruction Max, Emily and Matthew start to put out the mats in the circle corner. Once completed they run around the mats, bumping into each other deliberately and falling over with loud laughs. Justine starts putting chairs around the tables and the same three children run over to help.	WAL4 WAL9
09:00	Snack time arrives and the same three children rush to sit together at the table without any prompts. They sit impatiently at the table waiting for their snacks, fidgeting in their chairs, pushing at the table. Snacks are ready and Phil asks the children to sit sensibly before she gives them out and the three respond as one. Scotch pancakes and a cup of milk is given to each child. Max has finished his before everybody else has had theirs and asks, 'More, please?' holding out his plate to show it is empty. Enjoying his second helping, he drinks his milk in one go and again asks, 'More please?' Phil responds, 'Would you like more milk, Max? Say more milk please, Phil.' Max happily says, 'More milk please, Phil.' She praises him and tops up his cup.	WAL14 WAL6 WAL8
09:20	It's circle time and all of the children sit together on the mat. Phil gets their attention by asking, 'Who can point to their eyes?' and takes the children through different body parts. Max joins in happily, knowing all of the parts without hesitation. Moving on to nursery rhymes, Max is happy to join in with a selection of five popular rhymes, singing some very loudly.	WAL6 WAL14
09:30	The room is cleared to enable bikes and cars to be brought in from the shed. Max and Matthew play happily with lots of the cars/bikes, sometimes crashing into each other. Max is quite boisterous in his play and is often vigorous in his assertion to get the bike he wants over somebody else. Occasionally children complain, but not very much, and Max succeeds in getting his way on each occasion.	WAL10
10:30	The tables are put back into place and the children are encouraged to work in their groups. Max's group have planned to have a circle session with Joe, the nursery persona doll. There have been issues recently where one of the group has been quite domineering and has on occasion bitten in frustration. Phil introduces Joe to the group again and several of the children say, 'Hello, Joe.' Phil tells the group that Joe is a little upset today because one of his friends had just bitten him and he didn't know why. The children are all very sympathetic and Max is keen to give Joe a hug to help him feel better. Max seems concerned about Joe and is confident participating in this session throughout.	WAL2 WAL15 WAL4

A day in the life of Max Miller, aged 32 months continued

Time	Activity	Achieved
11:00	After this important discussion, the group are taken down to the pre-school room for a role play activity. Currently set out as the manager's office, Max selects a black jacket from the rack and hands it to Phil to put on for him. She offers to help him and helps him find the armholes in this adult-sized jacket. He wants the buttons fastened, but makes no attempt to fasten them for himself. As soon as this is done he realises that Emily has beaten him to the manager's chair at her desk and he shoves the chair out of the way. Emily doesn't seem at all bothered and allows Max to share her desk as she continues to 'write' a letter. Max gets himself a pencil and paper and writes alongside Emily. The children play happily, imitating work observed in Helen's office, including photocopying, shredding paper and making phone calls.	WAL6 WAL10 WAL11 WAL12
11:35	The children are enjoying their play so much Phil lets them play longer than she had planned so the children need to tidy up quite quickly. Max doesn't want to stop so refuses to help tidy up. He deliberately picks up the telephone and makes a call. Emily takes the phone from him and tells him, 'Tidy up Blue Room.'	WAL15
11:40	Phil quickly takes her group to the bathroom and encourages Max to sit on the potty before changing his nappy. She praises him for having a dry nappy *and* for using his potty and he is very pleased with himself.	WAL14
12:00	Lunch has already arrived in the room when Max arrives and he goes straight over to the table. He wants to sit next to Matthew, but there is no chair so he picks another chair and goes to put it in the small space next to him. Luke persuades him to put his chair back where he got it from and sit next to Leyleh, which he does very begrudgingly because his dinner has been put in that space. Using his knife and fork Max tucks in, leaving very little and not allowing himself to be distracted by anything until he has finished eating. He asks, 'More, please?' again, but this time it has all gone. He seems to accept this without any difficulty, puts his knife and fork onto his plate and pushes them away from him into the middle of the table. Pudding is brought in and Max manages this without any trouble. This time he is successful asking for more, but he is only allowed one extra helping, despite additional requests.	WAL14 WAL3 WAL4
12:25	After lunch Max goes in to the bathroom and washes his face very well, although he makes his sleeves wet in the process. Stella praises him for doing a good job and helps him dry his sleeves a little before giving him his toothbrush to brush his own teeth.	WAL16
12:40	Max is not very keen to sleep, but his mum has asked that he is encouraged to sleep. Stella lies next to Max and another child and encourages them to close their eyes while they listen to her reading a gentle story. Before long they are both asleep.	WAL2
1:40	Max wakes up when the lights are put back on and sits straight up, gathers his thoughts for a minute or two and then spots the sand tray. He jumps up still rubbing his eyes, and goes straight over to the sand where he promptly throws a handful at Josh who is already in there. Phil reminds him of the talk that they had earlier in the day about playing nicely with each other and Max smiles cheekily at her. He picks up a spade and the sieve and plays busily, shovelling and sieving sand over the remaining contents of the tray for quite some time.	WAL11 WAL15 WAL2
2:00	Group time. Max's group are due to spend this session in the sensory room so line up eagerly to go in. Max is at the front of the line walking to the room. He runs ahead and pushes the corridor door open. As the rest of the group catch up, Max has already taken off his shoes without undoing the laces and left them in the middle of the corridor. Once in the room, Phil turns on some light effects and selects a calming CD while asking the children to sit quietly on the mats. She talks to the children about the things that they are planning to do and starts by asking the children if they can crawl like a baby, which Max demonstrates immediately. They then move onto other more complex things such as hopping like a kangaroo (which most of the children including Max are unable to do, but enjoy) and slithering like a snake. Max throws himself into the activities wholeheartedly.	WAL7 WAL9 WAL10

169

A day in the life of Max Miller, aged 32 months continued

Time	Activity	Achieved
3:00	Snack time, but this time Max does not eat his scone immediately. Not even tasting it, he pushes his plate away and says, 'Don't like.' Not seeming to be bothered, he drinks his milk and waits for a piece of fruit. He selects a piece of banana, eats this and asks for another, which staff are happy to give him.	**WAL16**
3:30	Sitting on the mat to sing some songs, the children are invited to request songs to sing. Max immediately shouts out, 'Row your boat' and joins in very loudly when the others start to sing. Other children select songs that Max joins in with, but he declines the offer to stand up and sing to everybody else.	**WAL6** **WAL4**
4:00	It starts to snow unexpectedly so coats on (no time to practise our dressing skills this time) and out. Unfortunately the snow is very light and is not sticking, but Max enjoys running around trying to catch snowflakes. While he is playing, his mum arrives to collect him and is happy to watch him play while chatting to Phil about Max's day. Spotting his mum, Max is in no hurry to go home and smiles happily, but carries on playing.	**WAL9** **WAL1** **WAL2**

Code list	Additional suggestions
A Strong Child	
WAL1 Me, Myself and I	What shall we play with next? I don't like that!
WAL2 Being Acknowledged and Affirmed	I can be a good friend; Making up a story about our group.
WAL3 Developing Self-assurance	Helping to set the tables for lunch; Knowing what to ask for help with.
WAL4 A Sense of Belonging	Looking after our group teddy; Supporting a child new to our group.
A Skilful Communicator	
WAL5 Being Together	Why? This is my family.
WAL6 Finding a Voice	Talking about our trip to the library; What happens next?
WAL7 Listening and Responding	Learning a new song; What does that mean?
WAL8 Making Meaning	Talking nonsense; Beginning to use descriptive language.
A Competent Learner	
WAL9 Making Connections	Nature hunt in the garden; Splashing in puddles with our wellies on.
WAL10 Being Imaginative	Painting an exciting piece of music; Heuristic play.
WAL11 Being Creative	Making rhythms with our hands and feet; Touchy feely box.
WAL12 Representing	Symbolic writing; Letter recognition.
A Healthy Child	
WAL13 Emotional Well-being	Persona doll; Reinforcing our routine.
WAL14 Growing and Developing	How fast can we stop? Taste testing.
WAL15 Keeping Safe	The Highway Code; Supporting positive behaviour.
WAL16 Healthy Choices	What can go in our mouths? Dressing for the occasion.

Aspect title:	
Component title:	**Code =**

Development matters	Play and practical support

Sample activity	
Resources	
Health and safety	
Layout	
The role of the key worker	
Note	
Questions to ask/ suggested interactions	• •
Comments	

(P)   **Walkers, Talkers and Pretenders**

Completed by: **Date:**

Walkers, Talkers and Pretenders
(24–36 months)

Date of activity:	Supervised by:
Children involved:	
Comments	

Date of activity:	Supervised by:
Children involved:	
Comments	

Date of activity:	Supervised by:
Children involved:	
Comments	